Cavendish Legal Skills Series
2nd Edition

Drafting

Cavendish
Publishing
Limited

London • Sydney

Cavendish Legal Skills Series
2nd Edition

Drafting

Elmer Doonan, LLB, LLM
Solicitor, Wilde Sapte, London
and
Charles Foster, MA (Cantab), VetMB, MRCVS
Barrister, Inner Temple, London

Series Editor
Julie Macfarlane, BA, LLM, PhD
Associate Professor of Law
University of Windsor, Ontario

Cavendish
Publishing
Limited

London • Sydney

Second edition first published in Great Britain 2001 by Cavendish Publishing Limited, The Glass House, Wharton Street, London WC1X 9PX, United Kingdom

Telephone: +44 (0)20 7278 8000 Facsimile: +44 (0)20 7278 8080

Email: info@cavendishpublishing.com

Website: www.cavendishpublishing.com

© Doonan, E and Foster, C 2001
   First edition   1995
   Reprinted   1996, 1997, 2000

Doonan, Elmer
Drafting – 2nd ed – (Legal skills series)
1 Legal composition
I Title
808'.066'34

ISBN 1 85941 486 9

Printed and bound in Great Britain

Editor's Introduction

The essence of our lawyer's craft lies in skills ...; in practical, effective, persuasive, inventive skills for getting things done ...

Karl Llewellyn

The appearance of this series of texts on legal skills reflects the shift in emphasis in legal education away from a focus on teaching legal information and towards the teaching and learning of task-related and problem solving skills.

Legal education in the UK has undergone significant changes over the past 15 years as a result of growing concern, expressed for the most part by the profession, over its adequacy to prepare students for the practice of law. At the same time, many legal educators have voiced fears that concentrating on drilling students in substantive law promotes neither the agility of mind nor the development of judgment skills which provide the basis for continued learning.

Today, courses providing clinical experience and instruction in legal skills are increasingly a part of undergraduate law programmes. Both branches of the profession in England and Wales have fundamentally revised the content and format of their qualifying courses to include direct instruction in practical skills. In Scotland, the Diploma in Legal Practice, which emphasises the learning of practical skills, has been in place since 1980/81.

Nonetheless, legal skills education in the UK is still in its infancy. Much is to be learned from other jurisdictions which have a longer history of the use of practical and experience based teaching methods, lessons invaluable to UK law teachers, many of whom now face the challenge of developing new courses on legal skills. The ready exchange of ideas between skills teachers in the UK and abroad is an important part of the development process. So too is the generation of 'home grown' texts and materials designed specifically for legal skills education in undergraduate and professional schools in the UK.

The introduction of skills teaching into the legal education curriculum has implications not only for what students learn in law school but also for how they learn. Similarly, it has implications for the kind of textbooks which will be genuinely useful to students who wish to succeed in these programmes.

This new series of texts seeks to meet this need. Each text leads the reader through a stage by stage model of the development of a particular legal skill; from planning, through implementation in a variety of guises, to evaluation of performance. Each contains numerous practical exercises and guides to improve practice. Each draws on a network of theories about effective legal practice and relates theory to practice, where that is useful and relevant.

The authors are all skills teachers with many years of practical experience at all levels of legal education. They draw on relevant literature and practice from all over the common law world. However, each book is written specifically for students of law and legal practice in the UK and sets learning in the context of English law and against the backdrop of the Law Society's standards for the Legal Practice Courses.

Each of these texts is designed for use either as a supplement to a legal skills course taught at an undergraduate or professional level, or as a model for the structure and content of the course itself. I recommend the use of these books, therefore, to students and skills teachers alike, and hope that you enjoy them.

Julie Macfarlane
London, Ontario

Contents

Table of Cases

CHAPTER

1 General Considerations in Drafting

My words fly up, my thoughts remain below:
Words without thoughts never to heaven go.

Shakespeare
Hamlet

1.1   What is drafting?

Drafting – or perhaps more accurately, legal drafting – divides into
two main disciplines, namely, the drafting of legal documents such
as contracts, wills, trusts and conveyances; and the drafting of
pleadings, such as a statement of claim or a defence in an action in
breach of contract, negligence or some other cause of action.

1.1.1   Legal documents

The drafting of legal documents is concerned with the formulation
and preparation of documents that define relationships and set out
procedures which govern a transaction. The rights, benefits, duties
and liabilities which will, or may, arise from a transaction are set out
in a definitive form and the persons upon whom they are conferred
or imposed are identified. For example, a trust deed will set out the
rights and benefits conferred on the beneficiaries, and the duties
and liabilities imposed on the trustees.

The rights, benefits, duties and liabilities contained in a legal
document usually apply to a relationship between two or more
parties, as, for example, under an agreement, trust deed or
conveyance. The terms of these may depend on agreement
between the parties, so that, for example, in the case of an
agreement for the sale of a business, the seller and the buyer may
initially differ as to the content of certain important aspects of the
transaction and may eventually have to compromise on these if the
transaction is to proceed. Some legal documents are, however, the

unilateral act of an individual in relation to that individual's affairs, for example, a will or a power of attorney. In either case, the main object in drafting the document is to ensure that its provisions 'work', so that, when they are applied to circumstances to which they relate, they will provide clear directions as to what is to be done and who is to do it. This book is concerned with explaining how this objective may be achieved.

1.1.2   Statements of case

These were previously known as 'pleadings', and will no doubt continue to be called that. The term 'statement of case' is a creature of the Civil Procedure Rules 1998 (CPR). Statements of case differ from legal documents, in that statements of case set out facts and raise points of law which give rise either to a claim in law, together with any remedies or other relief sought, or a defence to such a claim.

Statements of case are intended to deal with contentious matters between two or more parties that do not appear to be capable of resolution without court action. Each party sets out his case in his statement of case and, in the normal course of events, the party starting the action (the claimant) issues particulars of claim and the party receiving the particulars of claim issues a defence in return.

Since the CPR came into force, the importance of statements of case has diminished. The protracted and expensive battles over technical pleading points which bought young barristers their first houses and bought more senior ones their second yachts are now unusual, and are usually permitted only when the judge has not read about the Court of Appeal's stern disapproval of such fun and games.

The CPR contains a number of guidelines for the drafting of statements of case, mostly set out in a Practice Direction to Pt 16, and these replace the old Rules of the Supreme Court. The main object of statements of case is to define the issues in dispute between the parties. For example, particulars of claim seeking damages for personal injury and related loss and damage arising out of a road traffic accident will set out the facts of the accident, the basis of the claim in law (usually negligence), and the injuries and loss sustained for which damages (and interest thereon) are sought. The CPR has swept away a lot of the old taboos which regulated a pleader's life – for instance, the prohibition against pleading evidence.

1.1.3 The structure of this book

The skills involved in drafting legal documents and in drafting statements of case differ in a number of respects and, for this reason, the drafting of pleadings is dealt with separately from drafting legal documents. Chapters 1 to 7 deal with drafting legal documents. Chapter 8 deals with drafting statements of case.

1.2 The objectives of legal documents

1.2.1 To provide written evidence of transactions

The main function of a legal document is to provide written evidence of the terms and conditions of a transaction. If the document records the transaction accurately and is signed by the parties to the transaction, the scope for fraud, forgetfulness or inaccuracy should be reduced.

In some instances, it is a statutory requirement that a transaction is set out in writing and signed by the party or parties to it. The necessity for such formalities dates back to the Statute of Frauds 1677, and it is still essential that many important transactions are recorded in writing and signed. For example, s 9 of the Wills Act 1837 requires a will to be in writing and signed by the testator; the Law of Property Act 1925 requires that a contract for the sale of land must be in writing (see s 40); a conveyance of land must be made by deed (see s 52); and a disposition of an equitable interest must be in writing (see s 53(1)(c)).

1.2.2   To prevent fraud

In those cases where statute requires a transaction to be in writing and signed, the main object is to prevent fraud. For example, if a testator could dispose of his property by making oral declarations, there would be a risk that those to whom he made the oral declarations might misrepresent his wishes (whether deliberately or otherwise) after his death. Although preventing fraud may be the main object behind drafting many legal documents, it is unlikely to be the only object. Evidence of a transaction may be required for other reasons, including those set out below, 1.2.3–1.2.6.

1.2.3   To set out future rights and obligations

If a transaction is to take effect at a future date, it is important that it is in writing; this will ensure that it will operate as intended. For example, a will will have no legal effect until after the testator's or testatrix's death and, therefore, it must be a full and accurate expression of his or her wishes. Similarly, a contract for the construction of a building should set out in detail what is to be done and how certain problems which could arise in the course of construction are to be resolved.

1.2.4   To record rights and obligations already conferred

A transaction may be recorded in a document even though it has already taken place, because it is sufficiently important to one or more of the parties. For example, the donee of a valuable picture may want a memorandum drawn up to record the fact that it has been given to the donee by the donor.

1.2.5   To set out the details of complex transactions

A transaction may be sufficiently complex that it must be recorded in writing if it is to be properly carried into effect and if there is a possibility of issues arising out of it at a future date. For example, it is prudent to have a written agreement for the sale of a large business to record the terms of sale and purchase and to set out any indemnities and warranties or other undertakings given by the parties. In this type of transaction, the terms and conditions are likely to be so detailed that it would be impossible for anyone to remember them or their precise contents. In addition, by reducing the terms to writing, many matters will be included which might not necessarily occur to the parties if they sought to rely solely upon oral discussion as the basis for their agreement.

1.3 Accuracy and legal documents

It is unlikely that a lawyer can avoid the need to sit down and draft at some stage in his or her career. In drafting, a permanent record is made not only of the transaction involved, but also of the lawyer's skill in legal drafting. Poor drafting skills may result in the record of the transaction being inaccurate and lead to unintended and often adverse consequences. Some common reasons for inaccuracy are given below.

1.3.1 Impenetrable language

The words used in a document may be the only evidence of a transaction many years after it has taken place. Consequently, they should be as simple and clear as circumstances allow. If they are long, arranged in unusual and complex phrases or antiquated, they may lead to difficulty in the interpretation of the document. Indigestible documents may require other lawyers to unravel their mysteries and, perhaps, the assistance of the court to determine their construction.

1.3.2 Ambiguity

A document which is ambiguous in some or all of its main provisions is worse than no document at all. It will lead to disputes between those affected by it and the transaction it was intended to record may not take effect as the parties intended, or may do so only after it has been necessary to resort to litigation.

1.3.3 Omissions

If important provisions are omitted from a document, it may be necessary to execute further documents to correct the position. This will involve expense which could have been avoided. In some cases, it may not be possible to rectify an omission by amendments, either because a party to the document objects, or because there is no power to do so. For example, if a written contract for the sale of a farm fails to set out a reservation of a small plot from the land being sold, it may be necessary to seek rectification of the contract in a court action.

1.4 Acquiring drafting skills

The traditional method of acquiring drafting skills is through articles or some similar apprenticeship, or learning on the job. Most practising lawyers probably acquired their drafting skills in these ways. In the past, these were the only ways that drafting skills could be acquired, as few, if any, courses were organised on the subject – it was hardly recognised as a subject – and there were few written guides on drafting. Consequently, the only sources for acquiring drafting skills were the guidance of an experienced practitioner, or what could be gleaned from books of precedents and their notes. The former were usually too busy to be able to give much of their time, whilst the latter are not intended to be teaching aids, but examples of documents and clauses that might be used in particular transactions. To some extent, precedents assume a certain degree of proficiency in drafting, because it will be necessary to adapt them to meet the particular requirements of a client.

Drafting, like any skill, can only be acquired through practice. A knowledge of drafting rules, although important, is no more likely to result in good drafting than a knowledge of the theory of music is likely to result in an accomplished pianist. Constant practice is required. Most lawyers regard themselves as good drafters, but executed legal documents are testimony to the fact that, as with most skills, drafting is practised at varying degrees of proficiency. A drafter is always learning and it is likely that, if he or she reviews drafts produced many years ago, some concepts would be expressed in a different way, and in some instances earlier efforts might be considered embarrassing. A drafter might also find that his or her drafting style has changed, and that matters which were felt in earlier times to be difficult to draft are now simple. This does not mean that the earlier draft was unacceptable or incompetent, but simply that the drafter is always learning through experience.

1.5   What is involved in drafting?

Drafting is more than a mechanical process of recording the terms of a transaction in writing. If this were all that drafting involved, it would not be necessary to look to lawyers to do drafting. Drafting involves the application of a variety of skills and processes to produce a legal document. These include ensuring that a legal document accurately reflects the client's instructions, that it takes account of legal and practical difficulties which have arisen or which may arise, that it is couched in words which are legally and factually accurate, and that it is well presented. Additional skills may be needed, depending on the nature of the transaction involved and the document to be drafted.

The manner in which each of these skills is applied will vary, since the content of a legal document is dependent on the client's instructions and the circumstances to which it relates. It is necessary to develop the ability to apply these skills in different circumstances and to recognise which among them deserves greater emphasis in a particular transaction. The major skills and considerations involved in drafting legal documents are described and explained in detail below, Chapters 2–7. The remainder of this chapter provides an overview of what is involved.

1.6   Client's instructions

1.6.1   Receiving instructions

The starting point in drafting a legal document is the receipt of instructions from the client. Sometimes, the client may give instructions which both he and the drafter know will require the drafting of a legal document, as, for example, when the client gives instructions for his will. In other cases, the client may not realise that a legal document must be drafted if his wishes are to be properly carried into effect. In the latter case, the client should be advised of the need for the document and given a broad explanation of its purpose and contents.

In most cases, instructions are received directly from the client. However, occasions may arise where they are received second hand through a friend or relation of the client, especially in the case of instructions for a will. In all cases, there is a danger that instructions obtained second hand may be inaccurate and, in the case of instructions for a will, there is the added danger that these may seek to promote the interests of the person who gives them. In all cases, instructions should be confirmed with the client before any legal document is drafted.

1.6.2   Obeying clients' instructions

A legal document must reflect the client's instructions. It hardly matters that the document is a model of grammar, use of language and technically correct if it does not achieve the client's stated objectives. For example, a client who asks for a will to be prepared under which all his estate is to be left to his wife absolutely, is not going to be impressed if he is presented with a draft under which all his estate is left to his wife for life with the remainder to his children absolutely. This is so even if it is felt that the latter would, in the circumstances, be in the best interests of the client. A document must be drafted strictly in line with the client's instructions.

1.6.3　Advising the client

If it is felt that a client's instructions are not in his best interests, he should be advised why this is the case at the outset and before any drafting is undertaken. If the client does not wish to follow this advice, the draft should be prepared in accordance with his instructions and a note placed on the file of the advice given.

In giving advice on the contents of a document, personal views must not be allowed to conflict with professional duties. Thus, if a client gives instructions for a will under which his girlfriend is to be the sole beneficiary, he may be advised of the consequences of not making adequate provision for his wife and children. However, if he chooses to ignore that advice, the will must be drafted as he has instructed even if it is felt by the drafter that his actions are morally incorrect.

1.6.4　Sending drafts for consideration

When a document has been prepared in accordance with a client's instructions, it should be sent in draft to him for consideration. He should be given ample time to consider it and, if it is complex, it may be accompanied by explanatory notes or an invitation to discuss its contents. In some cases, a draft document may contain more detail on a matter than the client desires. This may arise because the client is sent a draft which either sets out several options which could apply to a particular issue, in order that he can choose which should apply, or sets out exhaustively the provisions which are to operate in given circumstances. In the former case, there is little point in leaving the client to choose which option should apply if he has already clearly indicated his wishes on the matter. The likelihood is that he may conclude that his instructions have been ignored. The options ought to be left in the draft only if the client has not given instructions on the matters to which the options relate, so that he can consider the full range of possibilities which could apply in that case. In such instances, it is advisable to set out the options in a way which indicates that they are for consideration by the client, for example, by placing brackets around them or placing them in italics.

1.6.5   Deciding on depth

The depth into which a document goes should be adjusted in each case to meet the client's instructions. Too little detail may result in a document which is less than helpful. Too much detail may be counterproductive, because the client has indicated either directly or indirectly that it may jeopardise the transaction. For example, a client who has succeeded in finding a tenant for office premises he has been trying to let for several years may not want to upset the transaction by the inclusion of detailed provisions on rent reviews or repairs which might scare off the potential tenant. The client may be prepared to take a calculated risk on these matters. Similarly, a client who is negotiating a contract may not want too much detail on the circumstances in which the contract will terminate and his rights in those circumstances, including claims for damages. These might, in this particular case, impede a successful conclusion to the contract and, although perhaps desirable in such a contract in ordinary circumstances, cannot be desirable in this case if they would defeat the client's objectives.

1.7   Preparation and planning

The preparation and planning necessary before a legal document can be produced is likely to take up more time than any other aspect of drafting. The time required for this depends upon the nature of the client's instructions, the complexity of the concepts involved, the legal problems which have arisen or which may arise and on the experience of the lawyer doing the drafting. A great deal of time may be involved if the client is unsure of what he wants, or gives instructions from which legal or practical problems arise, which must be settled before any drafting is commenced. However, if the instructions are clear and uncomplicated, it may be possible to complete the drafting with a minimum of time spent on thinking through the planning process.

It is often not apparent from a completed legal document, especially to a layman, how much thinking time its preparation and planning may have taken. The quality of the finished document depends heavily on the thought put into its composition and design. Much thought may need to be given to how the client's instructions can be best achieved, especially if they do not readily fit within an established framework. For example, if a client has requested a transaction as a means of saving him tax, it will be necessary to consider the transaction from all angles before beginning to draft a document, and to test the transaction critically and the words which could be used to express it in the document. What should and should not be included in the document will require thought. What is excluded may often be as important as what is included. For example, in drafting an agreement, certain provisions may be deliberately omitted because they are not considered to be in the best interests of the client and in the hope that the other party to the agreement will not object when asked to approve the draft.

1.8 Anticipation of problems

Sometimes, a client's instructions may have inherent legal or related practical problems which must be dealt with at the outset, since they will dictate whether a transaction should proceed or determine how a particular aspect of the transaction should be handled. In addition to dealing with immediate problems, it is also necessary to anticipate potential problems which could arise from the transaction and to draft the documentation in a way which will deal with them. For example, the parties to an agreement may decide on a formula for determining the price to be paid for the exploitation of a copyright. The formula may be the result of detailed negotiations and its wording may not be open to alteration. If it contains the potential to cause disputes between the parties in the future, a detailed arbitration clause should be included to ensure that disputes are settled speedily and with minimum expense.

Anticipation of possible problems requires the application of both knowledge and experience. It will necessitate reviewing drafts critically, to ensure that they will be effective in relation to any potential problems which might arise. For example, in a trust deed, it may be necessary to ensure that the trustees have a discretion on matters which could lead to differences between them and the beneficiaries.

In many cases, a critical review may show that no serious problems exist, and the client may never, therefore, become fully aware of the time and effort this involved. In other cases, problems anticipated may be easily resolved. It is generally only when major problems are anticipated and discovered that the client is aware of this dimension of the work these entail, since his instructions are then sought.

Anticipation of problems may also require the exercise of care in the choice of words used to convey legal concepts. This will be especially important where the matters being dealt with in drafting are known to involve legal uncertainty. In these cases, it will be necessary to practise preventative law and to use words which will thread a careful path between what is certain and what is uncertain.

1.9   Use of language

The words chosen to express the concepts involved in a legal document need to be chosen with care so that they express the intentions behind the document clearly and accurately. Their effect must be considered both in isolation and in the context in which they are used, to ensure that they do not give rise to ambiguity. For example, if a lease refers to an obligation which 'he' is to perform without making express or implied reference to anyone who could be identified as 'he', it may not be possible to determine whether 'he' refers to the landlord or the tenant.

Many words have multiple meanings, and in drafting it is necessary to ensure that they do not cause difficulties. If a testator leaves 'all my money' to a named person under his will, this is likely to cause difficulty. It is unclear whether 'money' is used to refer only to cash, or in the wider, popular sense as referring to all of his property (see *Perrin v Morgan* [1943] AC 399). Again, the order in which the words are arranged will need careful scrutiny, since this may affect clarity. Thus, if a clause referred to 'persons who were divorced on 1 July 1993', it would be unclear whether it intended to refer to persons divorced on that day or persons who were divorced before or on that date.

The language used must also convey the concepts in the document to the intended audience which is likely to include the client, lawyers, other professional advisers and laymen. The lawyer will have to keep in mind that words and terms which may be clear to him may not be clear to others who may read the document. He will have to use language which seeks to convey technical concepts in non-technical, but precise, language wherever possible. Anyone who has had to grapple with the instructions on how to assemble a toy, or flat pack furniture, will need no reminding of the frustration which arises when these are written in a way which assumes that the reader is an expert. Sometimes, legal documents, especially old legal documents, are equally open to this criticism. These difficulties can usually be avoided by using simple language.

1.10   Refinement and rearrangement

Much time may be spent in welding together the facts and the law which make up the legal concepts in a legal document, and in choosing the words in which they are expressed, especially if they are unusual or complex. Consequently, it is not unusual for legal documents to require several drafts before a final version is produced. Sometimes, the words and concepts may come together easily so that few drafts are needed. Sometimes, the words and concepts may be stubborn and draft after draft must be produced. In the latter case, the problem may lie in the material to be drafted, as, for example, where a client requests an unusual provision to be included in a document. It may be felt that the first draft is too long and indigestible, and does not express some of the concepts in a satisfactory manner. A second draft may be produced to cut down the length and improve the clarity of the first draft. A third draft may follow if it is necessary to incorporate further instructions from the client or matters agreed with another party to the document, and a fourth draft may be needed to put a final polish on the contents of the document. Thus, in composing a provision which needs to go through several drafts, it may be that as much, if not more, material may be considered and rejected from the document as is included in the final version.

The end result of the process of refinement and arrangement should be a document which reads effortlessly and has an air of deceptive simplicity, so that the client or any other reader may not appreciate the effort and skill which was necessary to turn a complex mixture of law and fact into what may seem to be obvious ways of stating obvious points. However, in some cases, despite all efforts, it may not be possible to achieve the desired level of simplicity and clarity, because the concepts involved do not lend themselves to simplification or because pressures of time do not permit this.

1.11   Presentation and division

Drafting is not only a matter of collecting concepts into a legal document and ensuring that they are expressed in unambiguous words. It also involves the presentation of these concepts in a way which is logical and also meets with the customary manner of presenting documents of a similar nature. A legal document may, depending on its length, need to be divided into sections, clauses, paragraphs and sub-paragraphs so that the contents can be referred to easily on any particular matter, without the need for a reader to go through the whole document.

1.12   Knowledge of the facts and the law

It may seem a statement of the obvious that a lawyer should not attempt to draft a document in relation to a transaction or a particular aspect of a transaction on which he does not have a competent knowledge of the law. The danger is that important matters may be overlooked, with the result that the document does not achieve the client's objectives, and subsequent litigation may involve claims that the lawyer was negligent. However, a knowledge of the law relating to the transaction is, in itself, unlikely to be sufficient. It is also necessary to understand the practical aspects of the transaction to which the drafting relates. For example, a lawyer is not likely to get very far if he undertakes to draft an aircraft lease for a client, yet does not understand either the business of aircraft leasing or the law on aircraft leasing.

1.13   Review and amendment of drafts

The review and amendment of documents prepared by others in draft calls for as much in the way of drafting skills as the composition of such documents. This process may be necessary where an agreement is to be made between two or more parties, such as a lease or an agreement for the sale of business assets. The reviewer will have to deal with draft documents of variable quality and, in some instances, documents produced by laymen including the client. In reviewing, it is necessary to check a document thoroughly to ensure the drafting techniques and language used do not defeat its objectives, especially if it is known to have been produced by someone without legal training.

In the course of reviewing a draft document, it may be necessary to make extensive amendments, particularly to ensure that the clients' interests are properly protected. The amendments will have to be tailored to the style adopted in the draft document and, if it is poorly drafted, considerable time will be needed to pick up errors and to include any amendments so that they fit into the scheme of the document. The final draft must, of course, reflect the interests and instructions of the client, as one of the parties to the agreement. For example, a lease drafted by the landlord's lawyer will be reviewed by the tenant's lawyer, not only to ensure that as a draft it makes sense, but also to ensure that it contains all the appropriate terms which are in the tenant's interests and that it meets the tenant's instructions to him.

1.14   Use of precedents

Many drafting exercises begin with a precedent which is adapted to meet the requirements of a particular job. The pressures of meeting deadlines and of other work usually do not permit original drafting of most legal documents and, in any event, it would not make economic sense to do this. Many provisions in a document will be standard form provisions which do not need to be changed, and can be taken from a precedent. For example, the rules of a company pension scheme will contain standard administrative provisions which are unlikely to require change. Similarly, a contract for the sale of a house is likely to contain a large number of standard provisions which will not need change at all, or only in minor respects. In those parts of a precedent where change is necessary, it may be possible to make adaptations without the need for wholesale redrafting. It is only when the client requires something out of the ordinary that a substantial original drafting exercise will be necessary.

A precedent provides a good starting point for drafting, but it may cause difficulties if it is not used carefully. A precedent may be drawn from either a standard source, such as the *Encyclopaedia of Forms and Precedents*, or may have been developed by the lawyer or his firm. In either case, it is essential that the precedent is up to date and reflects the latest law and practice and, if it does not, to bring it up to date before it is used (see, also, below, 1.15). If a precedent is adapted for a particular job, it will be necessary to ensure that the words and terms used in any amendments are consistent with those already used throughout the precedent, otherwise ambiguity may result. For example, if a precedent for a lease refers to 'the premises', any amendments should not refer to these as 'the building'. The patterns of numbering and lettering and divisions in the precedent document should also be adhered to in the process of amendment, to ensure consistency.

1.15   Changes and updating

A legal document must reflect the latest developments in business practices if it is to be effective. For example, a licensing agreement for the use of copyright must take account of technological advances which affect the way in which copyright might be used, whilst a building contract needs to take account of any changes in building and construction practices. Similarly, it must also reflect the latest developments in the law and, possibly, those which it is anticipated are likely to come into effect in the foreseeable future. Thus, an agreement for the sale of a business must take account of changes in company law, taxation and employment law, whilst a lease will need to reflect the latest landlord and tenant legislation. Sometimes, the changes may be reflected in a precedent through the process of regular updating. However, it may be necessary to draft at a time when the changes have not yet been incorporated into the appropriate precedent, or to produce a draft on a matter where a precedent is not available, in which case original drafting may be necessary to reflect latest developments. This may not be easy if there is little guidance available on the legal implications of the changes and how these might affect a transaction and meet the particular needs of the client.

It is also important that the language of a legal document is changed and updated where necessary to take account of changes in terminology and to ensure it is couched in modern language. All too often, legal documents are filled with archaic words and terms which must puzzle intelligent laymen. Words and phrases are often used in legal documents when they could and should have been updated years ago. For example, many deeds still open the operative section with the antiquated words 'now these presents witnesseth that'. This might be better expressed as 'this agreement witnesseth that' or 'this agreement provides'. Similarly, in a lease, 'the rent reserved hereunder' might be better expressed in modern language as 'the rent under'. These matters are considered in depth below, Chapter 5.

The next chapter looks more closely at the process of drafting legal documents in relation to the two major stages of any drafting task: the 'thinking stage' and the 'composing stage'. It will start to translate into more detailed, practical terms many of the basic concepts and much of the advice outlined above.

CHAPTER

2

The Drafting Process

There is an art of reading, as well as an art of thinking and an art of writing.

Isaac D'Israeli
Literary character

2.1 From start to finish

This chapter considers the various matters which form part of the process of drafting legal documents, from the moment the client gives instructions which will require the production of a legal document, to the time when that document is executed. As drafting can involve anything from a single page document (for example, a simple will), to documents of 100 pages or more (for example, an agreement for the sale of a business), the complexity and time required to complete any particular stage of the drafting process will vary.

In all cases, the drafting process will involve two main stages, namely, the thinking stage and the composing stage. The former is concerned with analysing the material and assembling the legal concepts which are to be included in the document, whilst the latter is concerned with the actual preparation of the document. The time and effort involved in each stage may not be represented by the number of pages in the finished document.

2.2 Time

2.2.1 Estimating the time needed

The time needed to complete any drafting task will have to be estimated in advance, for several reasons. The client may request an estimate of the cost of producing the document (which may be based on the time it will take), or may indicate that the document must be ready by a given date. It will also be necessary to ensure that there is sufficient time to fit the drafting task within existing or anticipated commitments to other clients.

Sometimes, it is found in retrospect that an estimate of the time required to complete a drafting task had little relation to the time actually spent on it. Unforeseen complications may have arisen at either the thinking stage or the composing stage, or the client may have wanted to discuss the matter at greater length than was necessary or anticipated. With experience, it should be possible to estimate with a fair degree of accuracy how much time will be needed to draft a particular document and to deal with any problems which are usually associated with drafting that type of document.

Estimates of the time required for drafting are usually only inaccurate in the case of documents of an unusual nature, or those of which the lawyer has little experience in drafting. Although underestimates of the time needed to draft a document are the most common problem in time management, occasions also arise where drafting a document takes up much less time than was anticipated because problems which it was felt might arise in either the thinking stage or the composing stage do not materialise.

2.2.2 Time and the thinking stage

If the time needed to draft a document is underestimated, it is more likely that this will arise from problems at the thinking (rather than the composing) stage. The thinking stage may take up more time than anticipated because of unexpected problems arising from the client's instructions, or because the instructions involve complex legal matters. For example, a short will may require considerable time and thought because its apparently straightforward provisions need to be discussed in detail with the client and careful legal research is necessary before they are finalised. Sometimes, a discussion with the client may elicit additional matters of the 'Perhaps I ought to tell you' variety, which may put a different perspective on how the drafting should proceed and mean that time spent has been wasted, or that much more time than anticipated will be needed. The length of the document to be drafted is not an infallible guide, either, to the time which may be needed at the thinking stage, since a document may only be long because it contains numerous pages of standard provisions which have been adopted from a precedent, which will need little more than reading through to ensure their contents are appropriate and to adapt them to fit with the language and drafting style of the document (see above, 1.13–1.15).

2.2.3   Time and the composing stage

Underestimates of the time needed to complete the composing stage can arise for a number of reasons. Sometimes, it may be necessary to ponder over the choice of words to ensure that they reflect the client's wishes and are neither too narrow nor too wide in their scope. It may be necessary to read and re-read sentences and clauses to ensure they are not ambiguous or will not cause ambiguity elsewhere in the document. Cross-references in the document and references to provisions in other documents may need to be checked several times for accuracy, and clauses read and re-read to ensure they are not repetitive of matters stated elsewhere in the document, or do not overlap in some other way. The legal implications of the words used in other provisions in the same document and related documents may also require careful consideration. If it is necessary to attend to some or all of these matters, it is likely that the composing stage will take considerable time to complete. Furthermore, these are matters which cannot be rushed, as this will only lead to mistakes and omissions.

2.2.4   Time and experience

The time and effort which drafting may require will, of course, vary according to the experience of the lawyer. A novice may take days to produce a draft document which an expert could run off in a short time, because the expert is aware of the pitfalls that that type of drafting may hold and how they should be dealt with. It is also worth remembering that the opportunity to do the drafting without interruptions which break the train of thought will save on time, as interruptions invariably mean that the matters being dealt with have to be done over again.

2.3   The thinking stage

2.3.1   The client

The first step in the drafting process will be initiated by the client giving instructions. Some aspects of this have already been mentioned (see above, 1.6). Apart from those cases in which the client gives instructions which both client and lawyer assume from the outset will require a legal document, there may be occasions when the drafting process begins with the client seeking legal advice and, as a result of the client accepting that advice, a document may need to be drafted. For example, a client may start the process by asking for advice on whether he should enter a partnership. If, as a result of the advice, he decides to enter the partnership, it is likely that a partnership agreement will need to be drafted. The lawyer may be instructed either to prepare a draft agreement or to consider on the client's behalf a draft prepared by another lawyer, and to advise on its contents and make any necessary amendments to it.

2.3.2   Meeting the client's requirements

Since the client will initiate the drafting process by his instructions, it is essential that his requirements or objectives are ascertained so that any document drafted is tailored to meet those requirements or objectives. Sometimes, sufficient information may be supplied by the client at the time that instructions are given to ascertain his requirements. In some cases, the client's affairs may be well known to the lawyer, so that he knows what those requirements are and only needs minimum further information or confirmation. In other cases, the document to be drafted may conclude, and be the result of, detailed discussions with the client in which the possible contents of the document were considered with the client at length.

Occasions arise, however, where a client gives only outline instructions to draft a document, or supplies information which is insufficient to enable the draft to be completed satisfactorily because important information is missing. In the former case, drafting cannot begin until the client has given fuller instructions. In the latter, it may be possible to produce a draft on the basis of the limited information provided, and which is marked up or contains blanks in relation to matters on which there are either no instructions, or inadequate instructions. If the instructions are unclear on several important matters, it is normally advisable to discuss these matters with the client directly at a meeting or on the telephone before producing a draft, as it will require substantial alterations.

Without such a discussion, the lawyer will be drafting in a vacuum and it is likely that provisions will be included which the client does not want and provisions omitted which he does want. The likely consequence is that the first draft sent to the client for approval will need to be accompanied by a long letter, which the client may have neither the time nor the inclination to read, seeking confirmation on a host of issues and setting out the various options available in certain parts of the draft. The main danger with this type of drafting at a distance is that the client may fail to appreciate the significance of important points contained in the letter, or fail to answer them as fully as is required, so that further drafts must be produced and further correspondence entered into. A discussion with the client will enable many important points to be resolved and, in particular, the matters mentioned below, 2.3.3–2.3.7.

2.3.3   Obtaining the relevant facts

The factual background is essential in any drafting task. For example, it is difficult, if not impossible, to draft a will without details of the testator's assets or her family friends and relations. Sometimes, the client may be reluctant to disclose some or all of the details needed to carry out a drafting task, especially if they are personal details, and may need to be persuaded that it is in his interests to do so. Such details will be important in tax planning considerations, in advising on whether the dispositions requested have any disadvantages and in pointing out matters which the client may have overlooked. Similarly, it would be difficult to draw up a contract of service without knowing whether it was intended for a clerical grade employee or a director. In each case, different considerations will need to be raised to ensure that the contract is suitable for its purpose and, in the latter, it may be necessary to include provisions which would be wholly inappropriate in the former.

The factual background will also be important to gain an understanding of the circumstances in which the document being drafted is intended to operate. In addition, it may sometimes be necessary to refer in the document, either directly or indirectly, to important facts. One way to obtain the facts necessary to consider the transaction and to do the drafting is by using a factual checklist. This might take the form of a questionnaire which is sent to the client to complete. For example, a client who instructs his lawyer in relation to his purchase of a suburban house may be sent a questionnaire requesting details of:

1   whether the purchaser is buying as a sole or joint owner;

2   any sale to which the purchase is linked;

3   any mortgage which has or will be sought;

4   whether the vendor's sale is linked to any purchase by him;

5   whether vacant possession is being given of the whole property;

6   whether there is a garage at the property;

7   whether the driveway is exclusive to the house or is shared;

8   whether any outbuildings are included in the sale;

9   fixtures and fittings included in the sale;

10 the names of all persons who will occupy the property with the purchaser;

11 confirmation that the purchaser is not bankrupt and that no such proceedings are pending against him.

A more detailed factual checklist for drawing up a partnership agreement, depending on the size and nature of the partnership, might include the following:

General matters:

1   the name of the partnership;

2   the names, ages and addresses of all partners;

3   the nature of the business of the partnership;

4   details of business premises and place or places of business of the partnership;

5   the date on which the partnership is to commence.

Finance:

1   the manner in which partners are to provide capital for the business;

2   whether the partnership accounts are to include capital accounts and, if so, whether these will carry interest;

3   whether there will be any restrictions on withdrawal of capital;

4   details of ownership of goodwill;

5   details of any reserve funds required, for example, to provide capital for a sinking fund for a lease;

6   whether any partner is to make a loan to the firm.

Profits and losses:

1   the proportions in which profits and losses will be shared;

2   whether any partners will receive a salary out of profits before they are shared;

3 entitlement of future partners joining and on partners leaving the firm;

4 provisions on partners retaining outside receipts from, for example, directorships or consultancies;

5 the arrangements for drawings;

6 perquisites to be provided to partners, such as cars or accommodation.

Accounts:

1 the annual accounting date;

2 name of the partnership accountants;

3 how work in progress will be dealt with in the accounts;

4 details of partnership banking accounts;

5 details of insurance needed by the partnership business;

6 VAT arrangements.

Admission and retirement of partners:

1 arrangements for admission of new partners;

2 provisions for expulsion of partners;

3 provisions for retirement of partners;

4 the arrangements for dealing with the share of an outgoing partner;

5 whether incoming and outgoing partners are required to sign an election that the partnership is to be assessed on a continuing basis for tax purposes.

Rights and duties of partners:

1 whether there will be salaried partners;

2 whether retired partners can continue as consultants;

3 whether the partnership will provide medical, sickness and death in service insurance;

4   holiday entitlement of partners;

5   whether partners can take sabbatical leave;

6   provisions as to illness and incapacity of partners and maternity/paternity leave entitlements;

7   restrictions on outside appointments of partners;

8   duties of confidentiality to be imposed on partners;

9   restrictive covenants to apply on partners leaving the firm;

10 residential qualifications to be imposed on partners;

11 whether an arbitration clause should be included.

Management:

1   frequency of partners' meetings;

2   conduct of partners' meetings;

3   appointment and functions of senior partner;

4   appointment and responsibilities of managing or executive partner;

5   delegation of powers of appointing and dismissing staff.

Dissolution:

1   the provisions, if any, for partners to dissolve the partnership by notice;

2   provisions for dissolution of partnership on death, retirement or bankruptcy of a partner;

3   the arrangements for winding up the partnership affairs on a dissolution.

2.3.4   Legal and practical problems

If there are any legal or practical problems associated with the client's instructions, these must be pointed out and advised upon before the document is drafted. For example, if a testator wishes to appoint a trust corporation as the executor of his will, the cost involved may need to be brought to his attention and discussed, especially if the estate is small. Similarly, if a testator wishes to appoint his 16 year old nephew as his sole executor, he should be advised that a grant of probate will not be made to the nephew whilst he is a minor. If an elderly client has asked for his house to be conveyed into the name of his son, it will be necessary to point out the problems which could arise and suggest appropriate alternatives to the client, such as the possibility of his retaining the house during his lifetime, but devising it to his son in his will. In the first two of these examples, the advice given will have a significant impact on the contents of the document, whilst, in the third, the result may be that no document is drafted, or a document different in nature from that originally envisaged by the client.

2.3.5 Options

Some standard documents include clauses which contain several options available to the client as to how a matter should be dealt with. The lawyer may not, initially, have been given instructions by the client on which option he would prefer. Indeed, it may be that the client does not realise that he has options, or their significance, until they are brought to his attention. For example, a corporate client who wishes to establish a company pension scheme may not be aware that it is usual to include a power of amendment in such a scheme or address the issue of who has the power to amend the scheme. Should it be vested in the company or in the trustees of the scheme? Should it be vested in the company subject to the consent of the trustees, or in the trustees subject to the consent of the company? The lawyer will need to explain the significance of each option and, in particular, the potential liabilities to the company if it does not retain control over this power.

2.3.6 Time limits

The lawyer should raise with the client the time scale within which he is required to complete or produce the document. In some instances, the client may make this clear in his instructions. For example, a client may indicate that he wants to set up a trust before the end of the tax year so that the lawyer knows when the document has to be ready for execution. If the client has not indicated the date by which he requires the document, it is advisable to inquire, so that neither the lawyer nor the client is embarrassed if it is not ready by that date. In some cases, it is vital to the success of a transaction that the document should be ready by a certain date. For example, a client who has negotiated to purchase a business may be under pressure from the vendor to complete the transaction by a given date, otherwise the vendor will withdraw; therefore, the sale agreement must be ready by that date.

2.3.7   Consulting with other experts

In some matters, it may be necessary to consult with other professional advisers or experts because it is necessary to include technical information of a non-legal nature in the document being drafted with which the lawyer is not familiar. For example, in drafting a lease, it may be necessary to consult a surveyor on matters such as rent reviews; in drafting a company pension scheme, it may be necessary to consult an actuary on the funding aspects of the scheme; the lawyer drafting a share sale agreement may need to consult foreign lawyers if part of the business is carried on abroad. In these cases, the lawyer may often be able to suggest an expert to the client if the client does not already have a personal advisor. In any case, the client ought to be consulted and appraised of the need for expert input on particular aspects of the document.

2.4   Obtaining documents and papers

The majority of legal documents cannot be drafted in isolation from other legal documents, correspondence or papers. These will often contain material which needs to be included or referred to in the document being drafted. The documents, correspondence and papers required will depend on the nature of the drafting task, and it will be necessary to decide at the outset what documents are needed and to obtain them or copies of them.

In some cases, the client may supply some documents, correspondence and papers on giving his instructions. In other cases, it may be necessary to ask the client to provide some or all of the necessary papers. In all cases, the relevant documents, correspondence and papers will need to be examined with care. The supply of the wrong documents, correspondence or papers, overlooking a vital document or letter, the absence of an important page of a document or a piece of earlier correspondence turning out to be illegible, are common problems and cause wasted time and mistakes. All documents and papers must be checked as early as possible to prevent or minimise the impact of these problems.

In addition, it is advisable to ensure that any legal documents on which the document being drafted depends were duly executed and have not been replaced by later documents. For example, in drafting a deed of amendment for a company pension scheme, it is advisable to check that the deed to which it relates was signed by the persons who were then the trustees and that it is the current deed.

The need for other documents, correspondence or and papers normally arises for one or more of three main reasons:

1   The contents of an earlier document or paper may need to be reflected in the document being drafted because it sets out rights and obligations which it must embody. For example, in drafting an agreement for the sale of a business, it will be necessary to refer to correspondence and papers which contain important terms already agreed and which must be incorporated into the agreement. Similarly, in drafting the trust deed and rules of a company pension scheme, copies of any announcements about the scheme which have been made to the employees who may join the scheme and any booklets issued to them setting out the benefits of the scheme will be needed, as these will contain the basic terms around which the formal document must be constructed.

2   It may be necessary to refer to other documents, correspondence and papers because they set out procedures or terms which the

document being drafted must follow if it is to be effective. For example, the trust deed of a settlement will need to be referred to when drafting a deed of appointment of a new trustee. This is because it will be necessary to determine if there are any unusual procedures or formalities that must be adopted in making the appointment, who has the power to make the appointment, whether any consents are needed, or whether there are any restrictions on who may be appointed or the circumstances in which an appointment may be made. Similarly, in drafting a will which is to exercise a power of appointment in an *inter vivos* settlement, it will be necessary to refer to the trust deed of the settlement to ensure that the power can be exercised, that the testator can exercise the power, that it can be exercised by will, that the persons in whose favour it is to be exercised are objects of the power and that any conditions attaching to the exercise of the power are met.

3   The document being drafted may need to be dovetailed into the framework of other legal documents, and it will be necessary to see these documents to check that there is no overlap or repetition of their contents which could result in ambiguity or inadvertently negative important provisions in the earlier document. Thus, in drafting a codicil to a will, it is necessary to see the will to ensure that its provisions are not revoked either expressly or by implication and that the codicil does not cause ambiguity in relation to provisions in the will which it touches upon.

2.5   Legal research

Legal research may be necessary either as a preliminary to drafting or in the course of drafting. It is only in the case of very simple drafting or drafting tasks with which the lawyer is familiar that it may be possible to dispense with the need for legal research. In the majority of drafting tasks, legal research will be either essential or advisable. It may take the form of looking up precedents, statutes, cases or articles and commentaries.

2.5.1   Precedents

Research into precedents is advisable in a number of circumstances. First, when the lawyer is instructed to draft a document he has not previously drafted. Secondly, when he is instructed to draft a document he has previously drafted only once or twice, especially if that was some time ago. Thirdly, if the document is to include some unusual or complicated provisions. Fourthly, if the document relates to matters which are not familiar to the lawyer.

A perusal of precedents will give a broad idea of what the document should look like and its basic format or layout. It will give guidance on the matters which should, or might, be included (or omitted) and may, if it is from a book of precedents, include explanatory notes on the purpose of the precedent and its provisions. A precedent will also give guidance on the order in which the contents of the document should be arranged and how particular concepts might be expressed in it.

A perusal of several precedents and comparisons between their design and content may also assist in confirming or dispelling any doubts which may have arisen on what should be put into the document and how it should be expressed. Even if the document to be drafted is of a type which is familiar to the lawyer, a review of similar precedents may be advisable, especially if the document is to include some unusual provisions or is to incorporate provisions which reflect recent changes in the law. In the former, guidance may be obtained on how to draft the provisions and how to dovetail them into the other provisions of the document. In the latter, it may give guidance on how recent statutory changes might be incorporated in a concise and clear manner.

Although precedents can be helpful, they also present dangers which need to be avoided. A precedent may contain a provision which does not seem entirely clear. The temptation may be to include it in the document being drafted in the hope that it will have some purpose. The chances are that its inclusion will do more harm than good and it should be omitted. Precedents are drafted with certain specific situations in mind, and it is vital to determine the stated object of the precedent. Sometimes, it may not be possible to find a precedent which is tailored exactly to meet the needs of the situation facing the lawyer. The precedent will then have to be adapted. The lawyer should not get carried away and include a host of provisions which are neither relevant to the client nor within the ambit of his instructions merely because they look good.

2.5.2 Statutes

Reference to statutes will be necessary if there have been recent changes in the law relating to the contents of the draft. For example, a lease of residential property may need to reflect any requirements laid down by the latest statutes and regulations on landlord and tenant and, if the instructions come from the landlord, it will be necessary to take account of recent legislation which may impose obligations upon him or grant the tenant rights or options in relation to the property. Similarly, if there have been changes in tax law, these will need to be considered in a document which deals with tax sensitive issues. If earlier statutes have been consolidated, it will be necessary to ensure that all references in a draft are to the consolidating legislation. For example, a document should not refer to the Income and Corporation Taxes Act 1970, even if it contains a relevant provision which has the same reference in the 1988 Act and is in identical terms to that in the 1988 Act.

2.5.3 Case law

Case law may also have an impact on drafting. The court may rule on the construction of a particular word or phrase in a way which would require the lawyer to avoid the use of that word or phrase or to limit its use to a particular context. For example, it is clear from *Re Diplock* [1948] Ch 465 that it would be highly inadvisable to express a bequest in a will for charitable purposes generally by the use of the words 'charitable and benevolent', as these do not, as a matter of construction, create a valid charitable bequest.

Case law may include judicial comment on drafting practices of which the lawyer would be well advised to take note. In *Scarfe v Adams* [1981] 1 All ER 843, Cumming-Bruce LJ expressed his disapproval of certain conveyancing practices in the following terms:

> The facts of the present case are really very simple, but I hope that this judgment will be understood by every conveyancing solicitor in the land as giving them warning, loud and clear, that a conveyancing technique which may have been effective in the old days to convey large property from one vendor to one purchaser will lead to nothing but trouble, disputes and expensive litigation if applied to the sale to separate purchasers of a single house and its curtilage divided into separate parts. For such purposes it is absolutely essential that each parcel conveyed shall be described in the conveyance or transfer deed with such particularity and precision that there is no room for doubt about the boundaries of each, and for such purposes if a plan is intended to control the description, an Ordnance map on a scale of 1:2500 is worse than useless. The plan or other drawing bound up with the deed must be on such a large scale that it clearly shows with precision where each boundary runs ...

The lawyer will also have to take account of recent cases which deal with the legal issues relating to the document being drafted. These may either determine the course adopted in drafting or require consultation with the client and further instructions. In some instances, it may be apparent on reading a case that it will have little or no impact on the document. However, in such cases, the lawyer will at least have the satisfaction of knowing that it is not relevant. It is generally preferable to read a full report of a case, if it is available, rather than to rely on a summary in some newspaper or journal, as the latter may not go into sufficient detail on the issues that are important to the lawyer and, in any event, they are unlikely to set out the reasons behind the decision.

2.5.4   Articles and commentaries

Articles and commentaries may give guidance on a particular aspect of drafting. They may explain concepts with which the lawyer must deal and suggest solutions to problems arising from the client's instructions so as to help the lawyer determine what to draft and how to draft it. Even if articles and commentaries contain opinions with which the lawyer does not agree, they may nevertheless stimulate thought and help towards a solution to any problem involved in drafting a particular concept.

2.6 The composing stage

2.6.1 Preparation of an outline

Why make an outline?

The first step in the composing stage should be the preparation of an outline of what needs to be included in the document, especially if the document is being composed without the benefit of a precedent. The purpose of the outline is twofold.

First, it will avoid important matters being accidentally overlooked with the result that they are either omitted from the document altogether or are only considered at a late stage. If a provision is omitted it may, at best, be necessary to draft an amending supplement to the document or, if circumstances permit, to redraft and re-execute it. At worst, the document may be useless or damaging to the client's interests. If provisions are not included until very late in the composing stage, time will probably be wasted in grafting them into the document as references and cross-references may change, the order in which matters are set out in the document may need to be reconsidered, and consequential amendments may need to be made to existing provisions.

Secondly, an outline will avoid the possibility of concepts being fragmented, with the result that parts of the same concept are referred to in two or three places in the document, rather than in a single clause or section. For example, a trust deed should collect the powers of the trustees into one section rather than have them scattered over the document as incidental points in other provisions.

The use of an outline is often dispensed with in the rush to draft a document, and this can be evident in the completed document. One signal that the document may have been prepared without an outline is provisions which do not easily fit within the document because they are in a different drafting style and appear to have arrived in the document on a cut-and-paste basis. On further examination, it may be found that these provisions have not been properly cross-referenced or considered in relation to other provisions in the document so that they overlap, repeat or contradict other provisions.

What should an outline look like?

The nature of the outline will depend on the document being drafted. If it is a long document, the outline may take the form of a list of contents, with further notes on particular matters which must be included under each item, especially if that item is unusual or of particular importance in the document. For example, in drafting the rules of a company pension scheme setting out provisions on membership and benefits, the outline is likely to be divided into main headings and sub-headings. The former might divide the contents into six main sections, namely:

1 interpretation and definitions;

2 membership;

3 contributions;

4 benefits;

5 leaving the scheme; and

6 administrative provisions.

The outline may then detail the matters which need to be included in each main section. Thus, on membership, it may be subdivided into:

1 conditions for becoming a member;

2 procedures for applying for membership;

3 medical evidence and other information required with a membership application;

4 the circumstances in which membership will cease;

5 the circumstances in which membership will be suspended.

In the case of a short document, a detailed outline may also be necessary to avoid important matters being left out and to help with the organisation of the information to be included.

2.6.2 Drafting style

The second step in the composing stage is to decide on the style of language to be adopted in the document. Most lawyers will have a particular style of language which they prefer to use wherever possible. Whether a preferred style can or should be used in a particular case may depend on the client's wishes or on the nature of the document being drafted. A client may insist that the document exhibits legal formality or that it should be as simple as possible and avoid 'legalese'. The nature of the document being drafted may dictate the style to be used. The style used to draft the terms and conditions of a standard form agreement for the hire of cars and vans is likely to be different from that used in drafting a family settlement. Three main styles are identifiable in legal drafting.

(a) The traditional style

The traditional style of drafting is easily identified by its language and form. It is rather stilted and liberally peppered with words such as 'said', 'aforesaid', 'whereas', 'herewith', 'herein', 'hereinafter', 'thereof', 'therein', 'thereafter', etc. Surplus words and phrases are often used to pad out the document without adding to its meaning and good examples of this can sometimes be found in trusts and wills which use phrases such as 'The trustees are hereby authorised and empowered ...' or 'I do hereby authorise, empower and direct my executor or his executor or executors from and after my decease ...'. Unnecessary enumeration of particulars are not uncommon and strings of synonyms such as 'rest, residue and remainder', 'costs, charges and expenses' and the like are standard, as are longwinded provisos. The design of documents drafted in traditional style is characterised by long clauses which may lack punctuation or any form of subdivision, so that they may make difficult reading.

The following extracts illustrate the traditional style:

1   Setting out the parties in a deed of appointment of a new trustee

> THIS DEED OF APPOINTMENT is made the first day of January Two thousand and one BETWEEN JOHN FREDERICK SMITH of 1 Huggin Hill in the City of London, Solicitor, (hereinafter called 'the Appointor') of the one part and Robert Thomas Jones of Green House, Whitchurch, in the County of Hants, Esquire, (hereinafter called 'the New Trustee') of the other part.

2   Discretionary power of trustees in a company pension scheme for payment of death benefits

> The Trustees shall have the power to pay or apply any lump sum which may be payable under the Scheme on the death of a Member to or for the benefit of such one or more of the Discretionary Beneficiaries or to the personal representatives of such deceased Member in such amounts at such times and generally in such manner as the Trustees in their absolute discretion shall from time to time decide or think fit PROVIDED THAT in default of the exercise of the foregoing power by the Trustees within a period of two years from the date of the deceased Member's death the Trustees shall pay the whole or such part of the said amount remaining unpaid or unapplied as aforesaid to the personal representatives of the deceased Member and PROVIDED FURTHER THAT if the whole or such part of the said amount remaining unpaid or unapplied would or might vest in the creditors of such deceased Member or in the Crown the Duchy of Lancaster or the Duke of Cornwall as bona vacantia then the Trustees shall hold the whole or such part of the said amount unpaid or unapplied as aforesaid upon trust to apply the same to such of the purposes of the Scheme as the Trustees shall in their absolute discretion determine.

3 Clause setting out a life interest and ultimate trust under a settlement

> The trustees shall stand possessed of the said freehold property until sale and the sum of money and investments specified in the schedule hereto and the investments and other property for the time being representing the same (hereinafter together called the trust fund) upon trust to pay the whole of the income of the trust fund (including the net rents and profits of the said freehold property until sale) to the beneficiary during her life and after her death as to both the capital and income of the trust fund upon trust for the settlor absolutely.

There is still a demand from certain quarters for documents to be drafted in this style, since it is sometimes perceived as giving a transaction an air of mystique and formality. This might be the case in a will or settlement, but it is doubtful if this style has any place in a modern commercial document.

(b) Modern English

This style aims at cutting away the excess verbiage and long winded forms of expression found in documents drafted in the traditional style. It is based on the principle that the words and expressions used in a legal document should convey the concepts involved in language which will be understood by the audience at whom it is directed, but without sacrificing the precision needed to avoid potential ambiguity. The vast majority of modern commercial documents are now drafted in this style as, for example, business sale agreements and contracts of employment. The difference between the traditional style and the modern English style can be seen by comparing the examples below with those set out in (a) 1, 2 and 3 above. Each relates to the same matters and only the style is different:

1 Setting out the parties in a deed of appointment of a new trustee

> THIS DEED OF APPOINTMENT is made the 1 January 2001 BETWEEN (1) JOHN FREDERICK SMITH of 1 Huggin Hill, London EC4 ('the Appointor') and (2) Robert Thomas Jones of Green House, Whitchurch, Hants ('the New Trustee').

2   Discretionary power of trustees in a company pension scheme
    for payment of death benefits

> The Trustees shall pay any lump sum payable under the
> Scheme on the death of a Member to any one or more of the
> Discretionary Beneficiaries or the personal representatives of
> the Member on such terms as they think fit. If all or any part of
> the lump sum has not been paid out by the Trustees at the end
> of the two years from the date of the Member's death it shall be
> paid to the personal representatives of the Member unless it
> would pass either to the Member's creditors or as bona
> vacantia in which case it shall be held for the general purposes
> of the Scheme.

3   Clause setting out a life interest and ultimate trust under a
    settlement

> The trustees shall hold the freehold property until sale and the
> assets set out in the schedule below and any other assets
> which representing them (the Trust Fund) upon trust to pay all
> the income of the trust fund to the beneficiary during her life
> and after her death to hold the capital and income of the trust
> fund upon trust for the settlor.

(c) Plain English

The plain English style of drafting is characterised by the use of
words and phrases in a way in which their common or everyday
meaning is intended to prevail over any technical meaning they
may have. Traditional technical terms or reference to persons or
things are often dispensed with in favour of non-technical terms so
that, for example, in a residential lease, the terms 'landlord' and
'tenant' might be replaced by 'you' and 'your' as references to the
tenant, and 'we', 'us' and 'our' as references to the landlord. The
language used is often 'chatty' and, where words or expressions
have been used which might not be clear to a layman, they may be
accompanied by an explanation in brackets; so that in a lease, a
provision on forfeiture might begin 'You will forfeit (lose the right to)',
etc. The contents will usually be divided into short snappy
paragraphs with headings and use of bold typeface, underlining
and similar devices to assist the reader to digest its contents.

The plain English style of drafting is frequently encountered in standard form legal documents which are intended to set out the terms and conditions of a consumer transaction such as a hire purchase agreement or an insurance policy. The use of this style has considerable merit where consumers are involved, since the document will be of little use if it does not communicate the concepts it embodies in language which the consumer is likely to understand.

However, it is less likely that legal documents drafted by lawyers primarily for other lawyers will be in this style, as, for example, a business sale agreement or a will. One danger which may lie in the use of plain English as a drafting style is that it involves the use of 'untested' language. Although this style may be easy for a consumer to understand, there may be doubt whether it always attains the necessary precision required to avoid ambiguity. The following are examples of the plain English style and 1 and 2 below are the provisions in (a) 1 and 2 and (b) 1 and 2 above, drafted in plain English:

1 Setting out the parties in a deed of appointment of a new trustee

THIS DEED is dated 1 January 2001

PARTIES

JOHN FREDERICK SMITH, 1 Huggin Hill, London EC4 ('Appointor') and Robert Thomas Jones, Green House, Whitchurch, Hants ('New Trustee')

2 Discretionary power of trustees in a company pension scheme for payment of death benefits

The Trustees will decide which of the Discretionary Beneficiaries will receive a payment out of any cash sum which is payable on your death or they may pay it to your representatives. If they have not paid out all of the cash sum within two years of your death they will pay what they then have to your representatives. However, the cash sum will be kept for the Scheme if your representatives would have to pay it to your creditors or if by law they would have to pay it to your relations and you do not have any relations.

3   Extract from provisions in a standard form agreement for the hire of equipment

> 1   Words often used in this agreement:
>
> 'we' and 'us' means Hire Corporation plc
>
> 'you' means you the customer with whom we make this contract
>
> 'the Equipment' means the equipment hired to you in the Order Form
>
> 'the Order Form' means the order form accepted by us.
>
> 2   We agree to hire the Equipment to you to on the following terms. They constitute a contract between us and you.
>
> 3   We will try to provide the Equipment to you by the date we have agreed with you but we do not guarantee to do so and we are not liable to you if we do not provide it by the agreed date.
>
> 4   You must take the equipment for a minimum period of twelve months starting from the date of this contract. If this contract is a cancellable agreement under the Consumer Credit Act 1974 you can cancel it during the prescribed period, without charge.

2.6.3   The first draft

The method used to compose the first draft is usually a matter of personal preference. It will depend on the nature and complexity of the document being drafted and, in particular, whether a precedent is to be used as the foundation of the first draft.

Using a precedent

If a precedent is to be used, it will need to be read through at the outset to ensure that it is up to date and appropriate. The factual matters which are specific to the document, such as the names and other details of the parties, will need to be added, as will any recitals that are considered necessary. Unless the precedent deals with very simple or standard form matters, it will need to be adapted to meet the specific circumstances to which the document is to relate. This will normally involve three stages:

(a) Material in the precedent which is not required in the document to be drafted will need to be struck out. If it is retained, it will only serve to cause confusion and may contradict provisions which need to be added. At this stage, it may be found that the precedent contains provisions which may not have been discussed with the client. The options here are either to leave them in until the client is advised on them and can consider whether he wants them, or to remove them and raise with the client the possibility of their being included.

(b) New material will need to be added to cater for the transaction with which the document is to deal. This may take the form of removing provisions in the precedent and replacing them, because it is perceived to be easier to replace them than to fiddle around with amendments to the precedent or add in completely new material. When additions are made, the drafting style of the precedent should be adopted. Thus, for example, if the precedent is in traditional style, the amendments should not be made in plain English, as the effect will be as inappropriate as a mock Tudor addition to a Georgian house. The additions should also use the same system of division, subdivision and numbering and lettering in clauses as is used in the precedent.

(c) Existing material may need amendments either by way of minor additions or deletions. Blank spaces in the precedent may need to be completed and, where options are set out to deal with specific matters, it will be necessary to decide which option should be adopted.

No precedent available

If a precedent is not available on which to base the first draft, it will be vital that an outline is prepared (see above), and this may need to go into some detail to note all the relevant points which must be included in the first draft. The manner in which the first draft is prepared from the outline will be a matter of personal preference, and the main choice will be to compose it either in manuscript form or by dictation. Sometimes, it may be felt that the nature of the document is such that the first draft must be prepared in manuscript form. Whilst this is certainly time consuming, it can have the inherent advantage that material composed in manuscript is likely to need less in the way of amendment later on in the composing stage. This is because writing and speech are usually in a different form. Speech is usually in shorter sentences and supported by facial expressions and other body language, whilst drafting lacks these supports and must be more elaborate to compensate for their absence. On the other hand, for some, more familiar drafting tasks, dictating a first draft and having it put onto a word processor so that it can be revised in typescript is likely to save much time. With experience, it is possible to dictate the first draft in all but the most complex of drafting tasks.

2.6.4   Revision

Once the first draft has been completed, it should be put on to a word processor so that it can be revised from typescript. This will speed up the process of making and incorporating any further additions or amendments which may be needed. There is no limit to the number of further drafts that may be prepared and, if a second, third or a fourth draft is necessary, each draft should be numbered, dated and bear the name and initials of the lawyer who drafted it on each page.

The number of drafts needed will often depend on the degree of care exercised in preparing the first draft. Also, a factor will be the complexity of the drafting task and whether it is necessary to incorporate additional material on the instructions of the client or by way of agreement with another party to the document. Sometimes, composing a first draft may be interrupted by telephone calls and meetings, so that it is best to get what has been done on to a word processor and complete what may otherwise have gone into the first draft in a second draft. A first draft may, in some cases, become so complex with the number of amendments and additions made to an existing precedent that it is advisable to put these on to a word processor.

Even with simple drafting tasks, it is possible to go through endless drafts if a perfectionist approach is adopted, since there will always be small points that could be picked up and improved upon. In deciding if the document deserves such care that it may run to a fifth, sixth or even a seventh draft, consideration must be given to the importance of its contents, the significance of the further changes which are needed, the time limits which may exist for producing the document and the cost. There is little point in producing a perfect document a week after it was needed or spending £1,000 worth of time on a £100 document. In revising the first draft, the following matters will need attention.

Checking substantive provisions

The important provisions of the document should be checked to ensure that parts of it have not been accidentally omitted or transcribed inaccurately on to the word processor. If the first draft was prepared on a precedent or in manuscript, it should be compared with the typescript version.

Checking for clarity

Sometimes, on reading through provisions previously drafted, it may become apparent that certain matters could have been expressed in a more concise manner, or that they do not have the desired clarity. It is likely, in fact, that with every draft some point could be improved upon in some way. At this stage, the object should be to ensure that major provisions are in an acceptable form and do not lose their meaning through undue prolixity or poor arrangement, rather than fine tuning aspects of the draft.

Checking for effectiveness

The provisions of the document should be read critically to test them against possible circumstances to which they may have to apply. It will be necessary to consider whether, as drafted, they will work in those circumstances. For example, in drafting a lease on behalf of a landlord, it will be necessary to ensure that provisions for rent reviews are clear and workable. In drafting a company pension scheme, it will be necessary to ensure that the company has the power to terminate or suspend the scheme should it find that it is unable to meet the costs of the scheme for some reason at a future date. Certain provisions will need to considered together to ensure that they do not overlap, or that matters which should be included in one or other of them have not been omitted.

Checking for consistency

The contents of the document will need to be checked for consistency, especially if it was based on a precedent which was substantially amended. Definitions will need to be considered to ensure that, for example, two different definitions are not used to refer to the same thing or that matters to which a definition relates are not mentioned without being defined. Consistency in the use of terminology should be checked so that, for example, a loan agreement does not variously refer to the same thing as 'the loan', 'the advance' or 'the facility' or that a lease does not refer to 'the house' and 'the premises' in relation to the same thing. The manner in which the concepts are expressed in the document will also need to be considered, as differences in the language used could result in ambiguity. For example, references to 'he', 'she' and 'it' to refer to the same thing could cause confusion.

Check each section or division

If the document was planned so that provisions which have a common theme are gathered into separate sections or divisions, the contents of each section or division should be reviewed carefully. Check that the contents of each clause or sub-clause in that section or division, when compared and considered in relation to other provisions in the same section, do not overlap and contain all matters which are necessary or relevant.

Check references and cross-references

It is probably better to avoid references to provisions in other documents and cross-references to provisions in the document being drafted, if at all possible. This is because the contents of another document may change or it may not be possible to find it at a later date when reference must be made to it. Cross-references to provisions in the document being drafted can be a headache, as they are likely to shift if additional clauses must be added, so that it becomes necessary each time an addition is made to go through the whole document to check that cross-references are accurate. Unfortunately, on occasions, it is not possible to avoid references or cross-references. One way of reducing or eliminating the dangers of inaccurate cross-references is to add in parentheses the nature of the provision which is being referred to. For example, if a cross-reference has to be made in a trust deed to the trustee's powers of investment, it might be better to make the cross-reference as 'Clause 16 (Trustee's powers of investment)' rather than 'Clause 16'.

Check punctuation

Punctuation may have an impact on the meaning of the contents of the document and it should be reviewed.

2.6.5   The second draft

The amendments which may have resulted from reviewing the first draft will need to be considered in a further draft to ensure that they have been correctly incorporated, and to make a further check to see that they fit within the document. If the document being drafted is relatively simple, it is likely that, at this stage, no further work on it will be necessary; it may now be engrossed or prepared for execution. If the document is complex, it may be that some further amendments of a minor nature will be necessary. In a complex document, the opportunity may also be taken at this stage to give the contents a final polish. Whether this can be done will often depend upon there being sufficient time remaining before the document must be prepared for execution.

CHAPTER

3 Presentation and Division

Keep up appearances, there lies the test;
The world will give thee credit for the rest.

Charles Churchill (1731–94)

3.1 Importance of presentation

Legal documents are not often entertaining. Good presentation can help to compensate for unpalatable content. In addition, it is increasingly common for laymen to refer to and use legal documents, and, where this is likely, every effort should be made to ensure that the information is presented in a readable format. Consider the impression a legal document will leave if it is produced on thin paper, is closely printed in poor quality typescript, contains splodges and spelling errors, has unnumbered pages and long rambling paragraphs which are neither divided nor logically arranged, and lacks punctuation. Since the client will be expected to pay what he may perceive to be a substantial sum for the document, it behoves the drafter to avoid shoddy presentation.

3.2 Achieving good presentation

Good presentation can be achieved in a legal document without great difficulty; the following suggestions may help.

3.2.1 Paper

The document should be printed on good quality, white A4 paper. Documents printed on thin paper or in unusual colours such as pink may be difficult to photocopy and may also leave the client with an unfavourable impression. Longer documents should be printed on both sides of each sheet of paper, otherwise they will be too bulky. This is also preferable with shorter documents. Front and back covers should be used which are sufficiently strong to protect the document from damage. The front cover should identify the document in an appropriate way by stating the date on which it was made at the top, the names of the parties and the description of the document. The name of the solicitor who drafted the document is sometimes placed on the front cover. Thus, the front cover of a trust deed made on 1 February 2001 between John Brown, as settlor, and Richard Green, Fred Grey and James Black might appear as follows:

DATE   1 February 2001

JOHN BROWN   (1)

and

RICHARD GREEN

FRED GREY

JAMES BLACK   (2)

TRUST DEED

relating to

John Brown's Settlement

Underhill and Co
200 Cheapside
London EC2

3.2.2   Printing techniques

Many firms of solicitors have a house style for printing all documents. This is intended to ensure that the printing is of a uniform quality. The font used in the document must be of a size and type which will facilitate easy reading. The words and lines should be spaced so that the document does not look as if words have been squeezed into it in order to save paper, or given so much space that it looks like an infant's first reading book. In many legal documents, the printing is in the same style throughout. However, there is no reason why the size of the print or font could not be varied in order to improve presentation.

The use of capitals, bold print, italics, underlining and other printing techniques in a legal document is a matter of personal taste and their use may depend on whether they are permitted by a house style. Since these options are available as standard on virtually any modern word processing system, they ought to be used to improve the presentation of the document wherever possible. For example, definitions are sometimes printed in bold and underlined to emphasise to the reader that the word is used in the text of the document with a particular meaning. Thus, for example, if 'the Equipment' is used in a defined sense in a hiring agreement, emphasis as either 'the **Equipment**' or 'the *Equipment*' may help. Sometimes a proviso is emphasised by the use of capitals, as in 'PROVIDED THAT', to draw the reader's attention to an exception or qualification to a statement in a clause. Italics may be used to stress the importance of certain words within a clause, as, for example, an important date.

3.2.3 Listing contents

A list of the contents of a legal document of any length should be placed inside the front cover. If the clauses and paragraphs are given short headings which briefly describe their contents, a list of these with page references will assist the reader to find relevant material in the document without the need to go through each page. Thus, the list of contents for a settlement might set out as follows:

Contents

Clause	Heading	Page
1	Definitions	1
2	Trust for sale	2
3	Trusts of added property	2
4	Power of appointment	3
5	Trusts in default of appointment	4

3.3 Division of the document

An important aspect of the presentation of the contents of a document is its division into appropriate clauses, sub-clauses, paragraphs and sub-paragraphs. The object of this is to enable the information in the document to be referred to easily and quickly and to reduce the possibility of ambiguity. In addition, a system of numbering and lettering of clauses and paragraphs will be needed. The manner in which the document is divided will depend on its contents and the system of numbering and lettering used is a matter of style. However, it is probably better to follow a system of division and numbering and lettering which is well recognised, as it is less likely to impede perusal of the document. The following system is suggested in relation to the division of a document, since it is based on the method of division adopted in statutes.

3.3.1 Division into parts or sections

The object of dividing a long document into parts or sections is to group together provisions relating to the same subject matter in the same place. Consequently, the reader of the document can refer to the part or section concerned with some certainty that it contains all there is on that matter in the document and will, at least, make reference to provisions in other parts or sections of the document where these are relevant. Each part or section should be numbered using Roman numerals and given a heading to identify the nature of its contents.

This system is employed in legislation, and examples can be found in the Income and Corporation Taxes Act 1988 and the Insolvency Act 1986. The division of documents into parts or sections is mainly used where the document is long, such as, for example, the rules of a company pension scheme, in which the division into parts might be as below. In this example, only the contents of Pts I and II are set out in detail:

Part I	General
1	Commencement
2	Construction
3	Definitions
Part II	Membership
4	Eligibility for membership
5	Application for membership
6	Admission to membership
7	Termination of membership
8	Effects of membership
Part III	Contributions
Part IV	Retirement benefits
Part V	Death benefits
Part VI	Payment of benefits
Part VII	General provisions

3.3.2   Parts or sections should be divided into clauses

The division of a part or section into clauses is intended to arrange the material on the subject matter to which the part or section relates in a clear and logical fashion. The most important matters should appear in the early clauses and the least important at the end. Each clause should deal with a specific aspect of the subject matter. If the document is short, it may not need division into parts or sections, but only into clauses. For example, in a will, division into clauses will be sufficient. The division into clauses will depend on the content of the will, but the contents of a simple will might be divided into the following clauses in the following order:

1   Revocation of previous wills

2   Appointment of executors

3   Interpretation and definitions

4   Bequests of specific legacies

5   Bequests of pecuniary legacies

6   Bequests of annuities

7   Specific devises of freeholds

8   Trusts of residue

9   Administrative powers.

3.3.3   Clauses should be divided into sub-clauses to avoid length

Clauses in a document may run to considerable length, and, where this is likely, the contents of the clause should be divided into sub-clauses to improve presentation.

3.3.4   Sub-clauses may be further divided into paragraphs and sub-paragraphs

It may not be possible to present the contents of a complex clause within the limits of a main clause which has sub-clauses which set out either exceptions or qualifications, or other additional material relating to the main clause. This is because the contents of sub-clauses themselves may require exceptions, qualifications or other material added to them. In these cases, the further division of sub-clauses should be used, if this would help improve the clarity of the presentation of the material (see, also, below, 3.4).

3.3.5 Headings

Headings are now widely used to give a brief description of the contents of each part or section or each clause in a legal document. Headings will give the reader some idea of the contents of each part or section, or each clause, without having to read it in full. If headings are used to describe the contents of a part or section or clause, they may be used by the court as aids to interpretation. Since they are necessarily brief and may not always give an accurate description of the contents of the clause, it is advisable to insert a provision in the document that headings are for reference only and will not affect the construction of the document.

In choosing headings for each part or section or each clause, it is advisable to use headings which are as brief as possible and which are in common usage as headings for the contents of the part or section or clause in question. For example, a clause in a settlement setting out the trustees' powers of investment in broad terms should be headed as either 'Investment' or 'Powers of investment'. The heading of such a clause as 'Trustees' powers of investment and application of the trust funds' might be more accurate, but it is not sufficiently concise for the purposes of a heading. If it was headed 'Application of funds', this would not readily convey the nature of its contents to the reader.

It is not always possible to encapsulate the contents of a clause in a heading which is composed of only one or two words. In these cases, it is better to use a heading which is a brief description rather than one or two words which do not really convey what the clause is about. Thus, for example, a clause in a trust deed dealing with the appointment and removal of trustees ought to be headed 'Appointment and removal of trustees' rather than, say, 'Trustees', since the latter does not really convey the nature of the contents of the clause.

3.4   Paragraphing

3.4.1   What is paragraphing?

Paragraphing is concerned with the manner in which the contents of a legal document are divided into clauses, sub-clauses, paragraphs and sub-paragraphs. The systems of division and numbering referred to above will be dictated by paragraphing the contents of the document. In paragraphing, the object is to analyse the material to be included in the document and divide it into clauses according to its content. A broad division into clauses will be made so that material with a common theme is gathered into a single clause. For example, in drafting a trust deed, the powers of investment should be set out in a single clause. A clause which contains both the powers of investment and powers to maintain infant beneficiaries would be inappropriate and confusing. The material to be included in a single clause may be long and complex and virtually indigestible if presented as one amorphous mass. Thus, in paragraphing the contents of each clause, there will be further subdivision of the contents into their component parts. The document will reflect this subdivision by setting out the component parts as sub-clauses, paragraphs and sub-paragraphs, as can be seen in the examples below, in 3.8.

3.4.2   Paragraphing is determined by contents

In paragraphing the contents of a clause, it is essential to keep in mind that the subdivision is always determined by the contents. Any attempt to subdivide the contents to fit within a predetermined format is likely to lead to disaster. In addition, the subdivision should not result in unnecessary fragmentation of the contents, as this may be as unhelpful as presentation of the contents without any division whatsoever.

3.4.3   The effect of paragraphing

The main effect of paragraphing is that the contents of a legal document will be presented in a way which aids reading and understanding. In addition, paragraphing can avoid potential ambiguity which might otherwise arise. In many older legal documents, little or no consideration was given to paragraphing and the only divisions were by clauses. The clauses in such documents could run to several pages without any breaks, and the only techniques used to draw attention to important matters, conditions or exceptions were provisos. Sometimes, provisos cluttered the document and came in the form of 'PROVIDED THAT', 'PROVIDED ALWAYS THAT', 'PROVIDED FURTHER THAT', 'SO HOWEVER' or 'SO HOWEVER THAT'. The difference between a clause when it is not paragraphed and when it is paragraphed can be seen from the following two examples. The reader can judge which is the clearer and easier to read.

Example 1

Clause setting out conditions which must be satisfied for purchase of an annuity to secure a member's benefits under a pension scheme.

(a) Unparagraphed

25   Any policy or contract shall contain or be endorsed with terms to ensure that no benefit secured by it can be assigned and to show in monetary terms the maximum extent to which benefits can be taken in lump sum form either as commutation on retirement or a payment on death and to ensure that the policy or contract cannot be assigned or surrendered, except for a transfer at the option of the Member to another Insurance Company to secure another policy or contract subject to the same restrictions on assignment maximum benefits commutation and otherwise as the original policy or contract, or, a transfer of the proceeds thereof to a Relevant Scheme of a subsequent employer of the Member subject to the insurer certifying to the trustees or administrator of the other scheme the

maximum amount which can be paid out in lump sum form, or, a transfer of the proceeds thereof to a personal pension scheme subject to such conditions as may be prescribed by or under the Pensions Act or the Taxes Act, and to ensure that satisfactory arrangements are made by the insurer for the payment of any tax due consequent upon commutation.

(b) Paragraphed

25   Any policy or contract shall contain or be endorsed with terms:

(a) to ensure that no benefit secured by it can be assigned;

(b) to show in monetary terms the maximum extent to which benefits can be taken in lump sum form either as commutation on retirement or a payment on death;

(c) to ensure that the policy or contract cannot be assigned or surrendered, except for:

(i)   a transfer at the option of the Member to another Insurance Company to secure another policy or contract, subject to the same restrictions on assignment, maximum benefits, commutation and otherwise as the original policy or contract;

(ii) a transfer of the proceeds thereof to a Relevant Scheme of a subsequent employer of the Member, subject to the insurer certifying to the trustees or administrator of the other scheme the maximum amount which can be paid out in lump sum form; or

(iii) a transfer of the proceeds thereof to a personal pension scheme, subject to such conditions as may be prescribed by or under the Pensions Act or the Taxes Act; and

(d) to ensure that satisfactory arrangements are made by the insurer for the payment of any tax due consequent upon commutation.

Example 2

Power to mortgage contained in a trust deed.

(a) Unparagraphed

10   The trustees may with the consent of the Committee mortgage the Manor House and premises to secure such moneys as may be necessary for the execution of the trusts. No mortgage shall be made unless it covers the outstanding debt on the Manor House and premises at the time it is made other than (a) debts in respect of ordinary current expenses of the Manor House and premises and (b) debts payable to any person who consents to continue as an ordinary creditor after receiving written notice from the trustees of their intention to mortgage the Manor House and premises. It shall not be necessary for any mortgagee to inquire into the reason for any mortgage or whether it is for the amount of the debts outstanding or whether any person has consented to his debts continuing notwithstanding such mortgage being made and nothing in this deed or in any mortgage shall prevent the demolition or alteration of the Manor House and premises or the execution of the trusts so long as such mortgagee shall not be in actual possession of the property comprised or to be comprised in such mortgage.

(b) Paragraphed

10(1) The trustees may with the consent of the Committee mortgage the Manor House and premises to secure such moneys as may be necessary for the execution of the trusts.

(2) No mortgage shall be made unless it covers the outstanding debt on the Manor House and premises at the time it is made other than:

(a) debts in respect of ordinary current expenses of the Manor House and premises; and

(b) debts payable to any person who consents to continue as an ordinary creditor after receiving written notice from the trustees of their intention to mortgage the Manor House and premises.

(3) It shall not be necessary:

(a) for any mortgagee to inquire into the reason for any mortgage;

(b) whether it is for the amount of the debts outstanding; and

(c) whether any person has consented to his debts continuing notwithstanding such mortgage being made.

(4) Nothing in this deed or in any mortgage shall prevent the demolition or alteration of the Manor House and premises or the execution of the trusts so long as such mortgagee shall not be in actual possession of the property comprised or to be comprised in such mortgage.

3.4.4   Paragraphing conditions

A frequent use of paragraphing is to set out the conditions, exceptions, alternatives or contingencies in a clause. Thus, for example, if a clause is to give a named individual the right to exercise an option to purchase certain property at a fixed price, subject to a number of conditions, the clause should first state the power to exercise the option and each condition necessary for its exercise should be set out in a separate sub-clause.

Cumulative conditions

A provision may set out a number of conditions, all of which must be satisfied. The subject to which they relate should be stated first, and each condition set out in a sub-clause with 'and' following the penultimate condition, as in the following example taken from the Employment Protection (Consolidation) Act 1978:

8   Every employee shall have the right to be given by his employer at or before the time at which any payment of wages or salary is made to him an itemised pay statement, in writing, consisting of the following particulars, that is to say –

(a) the gross amount of the wages or salary;

(b) the amounts of any variable and, subject to s 9, any fixed deductions from that gross amount and the purposes for which they are made;

(c) the net amount of wages or salary payable; and

(d) where different parts of the net amount are paid in different ways, the amount and method of payment of each part-payment.

Alternative conditions

Where the fulfilment of one of several conditions will confer a right or obligation, 'or' should follow the penultimate condition, as in this example from s 53 of the Employment Protection (Consolidation) Act 1978:

(1)   An employee shall be entitled –

(a) if he is given by his employer notice of termination of his contract of employment;

(b) if his contract of employment is terminated by his employer without notice; or

(c) if, where he is employed under a contract for a fixed term, that term expires without being renewed under the same contract,

to be provided by his employer, on request, within fourteen days of that request, with a written statement giving particulars of the reasons for his dismissal.

3.5   Numbering of divisions

3.5.1   A system of numbering

A system of numbering and lettering of parts or sections, clauses, sub-clauses, paragraphs and sub-paragraphs will need to be adopted and adhered to throughout a document. The purpose of numbering and lettering is to enable provisions to be referred to easily, especially if they are set out in a list of contents at the beginning of the document. In longer documents, this system will also be required, so that unavoidable cross-references can be made to other provisions in the document. Only one system should be used throughout the document, otherwise the document will have the appearance of being cobbled together from several sources and will have meaningless or confusing cross-references.

In shorter documents, the numbering and lettering system is likely to be simple and it may be that numbers only will be sufficient. However, in complex documents, a detailed system of numbering and lettering will be needed to ensure that there is no repetition within the system which would lead to confusion. This might arise if, for example, the main clauses were numbered as 1, 2, 3, etc, sub-clauses as (a), (b), (c) etc and paragraphs in the sub-clauses as 1, 2, 3, etc. If this system were used, a cross-reference in a clause which stated 'see 1 above' could refer to clause 1 or to para 1 in the clause in which the reference was made, if that clause contained a para 1, and the content of the clauses may not be able to resolve the ambiguity. The system adopted must be such that there is no repetition of the same style of numbers and letters in any clauses, sub-clauses, paragraphs or sub-paragraphs. The two systems commonly used to number and letter divisions are set out below, in 3.5.2 and 3.5.3. Whether one or the other is used is a matter of taste.

3.5.2   Legislative drafting system

The method of numbering and lettering sections, sub-sections, clauses and paragraphs in statutes and statutory instruments is well settled and is, in itself, likely to avoid the possibility of confusion if it is properly adapted for use in legal documents. It might be adapted as follows:

Parts or sections

These are numbered with Roman numerals with a short heading in capitals. For example:

PART I   DEFINITIONS

PART X   TERMINATION

Clauses

These should be numbered consecutively using Arabic numerals and given a short heading. For example:

PART IV   POWERS OF TRUSTEES

    5   Powers to Delegate

Sub-clauses

These are numbered consecutively using Arabic numerals in parentheses. Short headings may be used for sub-clauses, but this is a matter of discretion. For example:

5   Powers to Delegate

   (1) Appointment of Administrator

Paragraphs

These are given letters of the alphabet in lower case and in parentheses. For example:

5   Powers to Delegate

   (1) Appointment of Administrator

     (a) The trustees may appoint ...

Sub-paragraphs

These are numbered consecutively, in small Roman numerals in parentheses. For example:

5   Powers to Delegate

   (1) Appointment of Administrator

      (a) The trustees may appoint an administrator subject to the following conditions:

         (i)   he must be a member of ...

Sub-sub paragraphs

A division of a document down to sub-paragraphs will normally be sufficient in most cases. If further division is required, they should be lettered with capital letters in parentheses. For example:

5   Powers to Delegate

   (1) Appointment of Administrator

      (a) The trustees may appoint an administrator subject to the following conditions:

         (i)   he must be a member of either:

            (A) the Institute of ...

Sub-sub-sub paragraphs

These are numbered with large Roman numerals in parentheses. For example:

5   Powers to Delegate

   (1) Appointment of Administrator

      (a) The trustees may appoint an administrator subject to the following conditions:

         (i)   He must be a member of either:

            (A) the Institute of ... and

               (I) ...

Experience is likely to show that too much subdivision can be as irritating to the reader as too little. It will rarely be necessary to subdivide the document beyond sub-paragraphs. If a draft requires this, it may be appropriate to reconsider the manner in which its contents have been divided in order to see if it might be avoided. A common reason for excessive subdivision is that too little is placed in paragraphs and sub-paragraphs, and further division is of matters that could have been condensed together in a single clause or paragraph without affecting the content or clarity.

3.5.3   Decimal drafting system

This system uses numbers with decimal points. The main clauses are numbered consecutively and each sub-clause is denoted by the addition of a decimal point and a further number. The system appears to originate from the Dewey decimal system, which was developed for library cataloguing purposes. There are a number of variations in its application, but a common method is illustrated by the following example:

9   Powers to Delegate

   9.1 Appointment of Administrator

      9.1.1   The trustees may appoint an administrator subject to the following conditions:

         9.1.1.1   the administrator must be:

           9.1.1.1.1   a British citizen who is: ...

The decimal system is satisfactory for documents where subdivision will not require more than three decimal points, as, for example, 9.1.1.1 above. Beyond this, the decimal system is liable to become confusing, especially if there is a need to make a number of cross-references in the document, and it is sometimes abandoned at this stage in favour of lettering so that further divisions are lettered as (a), (b), (c), etc, or (i), (ii), (iii), etc.

3.6   Schedules

Many legal documents, especially those of some length, have schedules appended to them containing material which is relevant to clauses in the document. Whether a schedule is used will depend on the nature of the material. Schedules are used for the following purposes.

3.6.1   To set out detailed provisions

It may be inconvenient to incorporate lengthy and detailed provisions into one or more clauses in a document. This may be for several reasons. The detailed provisions may not be similar in nature to the contents of the clauses. For example, the rules of a company pension scheme which enjoys Inland Revenue approval must set out limitations on the maximum benefits that the scheme can provide. These limits are lengthy and complex, and are better set out in a schedule to the rules than in the rules themselves. An agreement for the sale of business assets or shares in a company is likely to contain several schedules which contain material that could not be set out in the agreement without making it unnecessarily complex. For example, in a share sale agreement, schedules may be appended to the agreement which contain the following:

- the names and addresses of the vendors and the number of shares they are selling, especially if there are numerous vendors;

- details of the company, including the date of incorporation, registered number, registered office, directors, secretary, accounting reference date, authorised share capital, issued and allotted share capital, details of subsidiary companies, etc;

- warranties and undertakings relating to capital and distribution, accounts, property, assets, business and trading, employees and pensions, taxation, environmental matters, disputes, title to shares, etc;

- details of freehold and leasehold properties of the company.

3.6.2   To include copies of documents

It may sometimes be necessary or prudent to set out a copy of another document in a schedule where that other document is relevant to the contents of the document to which it is appended. For example, a share sale agreement may contain copies of letters of resignation of the directors of the company prior to the sale, or agreements that the vendors undertake not to enter into competition with the business they are selling to the purchaser. A conveyance may contain a map which identifies the property conveyed. A building contract may have a schedule which contains architects' drawings and specifications of the property to be constructed and a settlement may contain a copy of an earlier settlement if it is a resettlement of property from that earlier settlement.

3.6.3   To list items

A list of items or the names of persons may be inappropriate in the body of a document and better contained within a schedule. For example, if a settlor is establishing a settlement of various shares, chattels and real property, it is likely to be more convenient to set these out in a schedule. A declaration of the trusts in the deed which stated that the settlor settled upon trust his 100 shares in ICI, 1,000 shares in BP, 5,000 shares in BG, his stamp collection, his vintage motor car, his Rolex watch, his holiday villa, his timeshare in Spain, his house in London, etc, etc, could well end up like the particulars of an auction sale. It is better to state that the settlor settles upon trust the property referred to in the schedule and give full particulars of the property settled in that schedule.

3.6.4   To set out examples

A clause which confers rights may sometimes be supplemented by provisions in a schedule which illustrate by way of example how those provisions are to be applied in practice. For example, the rules of a company pension scheme may contain a schedule which illustrates how a pension is calculated and the manner in which it may be increased whilst in payment. The use of examples can also be found in schedules to statutes as a way of showing how certain sections are to operate; see, for example, Sched 2, Pt II of the Consumer Credit Act 1974.

If it is considered appropriate to incorporate material in a schedule to a document, the manner in which it is presented and divided will be similar to that used for the main document (see above, 3.3–3.4). However, it is worthwhile indicating at the beginning of the schedule the clause in the document to which it relates for ease of reference and to avoid possible ambiguity. For example, if Sched 1 in a trust deed related to cl 10 in that deed, which stated that the administrative powers of the trustees were set out in that schedule, it ought to begin:

SCHEDULE 1

(Clause 10)

Administrative Powers of the Trustees

3.7   Tables

Tables can be used to set out technical data in a document more clearly than words. Unfortunately, there is often a tendency to avoid the use of tables, possibly on the misguided basis that they do not constitute real drafting. If information can be presented more effectively in a table rather than a long narrative, a table should be used, as the object of a document is to communicate information by the most effective means to the reader. For example, a partnership agreement may contain a schedule which sets out the manner in which profits are to be divided between the partners in the first four years after the formation of the partnership. The use of a table to present this information is more effective than a narrative, as the following examples illustrate.

3.7.1   Narrative form

SCHEDULE 2

(Clause 11)

Division of Profits

The Profits shall be divided between the Partners in the percentages shown below in each of the Financial Years of the Partnership as follows:

1993/94   Brown shall receive 45%, Green shall receive 30%, Black shall receive 15% and Grey shall receive 10%.

1994/95   Brown shall receive 40%, Green shall receive 30%, Black shall receive 20% and Grey shall receive 10%.

1995/96   Brown shall receive 35%, Green shall receive 25%, Black shall receive 25% and Grey shall receive 15%.

In subsequent years Brown shall receive 30%, Green shall receive 25%, Black shall receive 25% and Grey shall receive 20%.

3.7.2   Tabular form

SCHEDULE 2

(Clause 11)

Division of Profits

The Profits shall be divided between the Partners in the percentages shown below in each of the Financial Years of the Partnership as follows:

	1993/94	1994/95	1995/96	Subsequent Years
Brown	45%	40%	35%	30%
Green	30%	30%	25%	25%
Black	15%	20%	25%	25%
Grey	10%	10%	15%	20%

The use of a table can avoid potential ambiguity which might creep into presentation of information in narrative form. Sometimes, the information may be such that the only sensible method of presentation is in tabular form. For example, if the rules of a company pension scheme indicate the amount of pension a member can take in a cash lump sum, the obvious way to do this is in a table:

Years of service at Normal Retirement Date	Maximum lump sum expressed as 80ths of Final Remuneration
1–8	3 for each year
9	30
10	36
11	42
12	48
13	54
14	63
15	72
16	81
17	90
18	99
19	108
20 or more years	120

If a table is liable to alter because, for example, its contents are based on statutory provisions or are dependent upon a given set of circumstances continuing, it may be advisable to put the table in a schedule to the document, as this will enable the table to be changed without the need to re-execute the document. If this is desired, it will be necessary to ensure that the document permits this by drafting the clause that refers to the table in terms which state that the relevant data is to be found in the table as updated or amended from time to time.

3.8 Enumerations

3.8.1 What is an enumeration?

Sometimes, a clause may contain a list of names or items in the form of contingencies, alternatives or conditions which must be satisfied if a right or privilege is to be conferred or a duty or obligation imposed. This is an enumeration. In drafting an enumeration, each item should be set out in a separate clause or sub-clause. An enumeration may be presented as a single paragraph without division, but in this form, as can be seen in the examples above, 3.4.3, it is likely to be difficult to comprehend and could, in some instances, result in ambiguity.

3.8.2 Rules for drafting an enumeration

In drafting an enumeration, the following rules should be observed:

• All items in the enumeration should belong to the same class.

A clause in a will may direct the payment of pecuniary legacies of £5,000 each to 10 named persons. As the 10 named persons all belong to the same class, they can be dealt with in a single clause. One way in which the clause could be drafted is:

> I direct my executors to pay the sum of £5,000 to each of John Smith, Peter Smith, Mary Smith, John Jones, Alfred Jones, James Jones, Ann Brown, Jane Brown, Thomas Green and Betty Green.

The enumeration of the named pecuniary legatees might, however, be better presented by placing their names in sub-clauses, as follows:

> I direct my executors to pay the sum of £5,000 to each of:
>
> (1) John Smith;
>
> (2) Peter Smith;
>
> (3) Mary Smith;
>
> (4) John Jones;
>
> (5) Alfred Jones;

(6) James Jones;

(7) Ann Brown;

(8) Jane Brown;

(9) Thomas Green;

(10) Betty Green.

In this example, the presentation of each legatee's name in a separate sub-clause also leaves room for the inclusion of that legatee's address, if it was felt this would avoid any ambiguity as to the identity of the beneficiary, as, for example, where the beneficiary has a relative of the same name who might claim that he is the intended legatee.

A clause should not mix items from different classes, as this could to lead to ambiguity. If, in the example above, the testator intended to leave £10,000 to Betty Green, sub-cl (10) should not be 'Betty Green who shall receive £10,000'. This does not belong in a clause giving £5,000 legacies and, in any event, this legacy is not responsive to the introductory words; it therefore breaches 2, below. The better course would be to deal with Betty Green's pecuniary legacy in a separate clause or, if appropriate, in a clause where other pecuniary legacies of £10,000 are made.

- If an enumeration begins with introductory words, each item in the enumeration should be relevant to those words.

An example of this is s 5(2) of the Nurses, Midwives and Health Visitors Act 1979. This states:

A National Board shall consist of:

(a) a chairman appointed by the Secretary of State from among persons who are registered nurses, midwives or health visitors,

(b) such number of other members appointed by the Secretary of State as he may specify by order,

(c) the person for the time being appointed in pursuance of sub-section (6)(a) to be the chief executive officer of the Board, and

    (d) any person for the time being appointed in pursuance of sub-section (6)(b) to an office under the Board which is specified for the purposes of this paragraph by the Secretary of State by order.

- If a sentence containing an enumeration continues beyond the enumeration, the words beyond the enumeration should be relevant to each item in the enumeration.

An example of this is to be found in s 66(2) of the Consumer Credit Act 1974, which provides:

    (2) The debtor accepts a credit-token when:

        (a) it is signed, or

        (b) a receipt for it is signed, or

        (c) it is first used,

        either by the debtor himself or by a person who, pursuant to the agreement, is authorised by him to use it.

- An enumeration should be indented from the material which precedes or follows it.

The object of this is to assist clarity and enable the reader to distinguish readily between an enumeration and an enumeration within an enumeration, as in the following example from s 1 of the Employment Protection (Consolidation) Act 1978:

    (4) Subject to sub-section (5), every statement given to an employee under this section shall include a note –

        (a) specifying any disciplinary rules applicable to the employee, or referring to a document which is reasonably accessible to the employee and which specifies such rules;

        (b) specifying, by description or otherwise –

        (i) a person to whom the employee can apply if he is dissatisfied with any disciplinary decision relating to him; and

        (ii) a person to whom the employee can apply for the purpose of seeking redress of any grievance relating to his employment;

(c) where there are further steps consequent upon any such application, explaining those steps or referring to a document which is reasonably accessible to the employee and which explains them; and

(d) stating whether a contracting-out certificate is in force for the employment in respect of which the statement is given.

• The penultimate item in an enumeration should be followed by 'and' or 'or' if the sentence containing the enumeration continues beyond the enumeration.

Sometimes, 'and' or 'or' may follow each item in an enumeration in order to leave no doubt that the items are alternatives or cumulative. An example of the former is to be found in s 18 of the Human Fertilisation and Embryology Act 1990. An example of the latter is s 9 of the Wills Act 1837. These state:

18(1) A licence committee may revoke a licence if it is satisfied:

(a) that any information given for the purposes of the application for the grant of the licence was in any material respect false or misleading;

(b) that the premises to which the licence relates are no longer available;

(c) that the person responsible has failed to discharge, or is unable because of incapacity to discharge, the duty under s 17 of this Act or has failed to comply with directions given in connection with any licence; or

(d) that there has been any other material change of circumstances since the licence was granted.

9 No will shall be valid unless –

(a) it is in writing, and signed by the testator, or by some other person in his presence and by his direction; and

(b) it appears that the testator intended by his signature to give effect to the will; and

(c) the signature is made or acknowledged by the testator in the presence of two or more witnesses present at the same time; and

(d) each witness either –

(i) attests and signs the will; or

(ii) acknowledges his signature,

in the presence of the testator (but not necessarily in the presence of any other witness),

but no form of attestation shall be necessary.

- If the enumeration is a single list following a sentence which ends with the enumeration, the penultimate item should not be followed by 'and' or 'or'

An example of this is to be found in s 1(3) of the Fatal Accidents Act 1976, which sets out the definition of 'dependant' for the purposes of that Act. It states:

(3) In this Act 'dependant' means –

(a) the wife or husband or former wife or husband of the deceased;

(b) any person who –

(i) was living with the deceased in the same household immediately before the date of death; and

(ii) had been living with the deceased in the same household for at least two years before that date; and

(iii) was living during the whole of that period as the husband or wife of the deceased;

(c) any parent or other ascendant of the deceased;

(d) any person who was treated by the deceased as his parent;

(e) any child or other descendant of the deceased;

(f) any person (not being a child of the deceased) who, in the case of any marriage to which the deceased was at any time a party, was treated by the deceased as a child of the family in relation to that marriage;

(g) any person who is, or is the issue of, a brother, sister, uncle or aunt of the deceased.

3.9   Maps, plans and diagrams

Consideration should be given to the inclusion of a map, plan or diagram in a document where this would assist the reader to understand the concepts which are dealt with by the document. It is likely that, in some transactions, a map, plan or diagram will convey matters much more easily and clearly than any statement.

3.9.1   Maps

Maps may be used in legal documents which deal with property. For example, in a contract for the sale of land, a map will help to indicate the property which is the subject matter of the contract. A map may also be used to indicate easements such as a right of way, rights to shooting, etc, and the course of pipes and cables. If a map is used to indicate rights and obligations, it should be of a scale which is sufficient to leave no doubt as to the property which is involved (see *Scarfe v Adams* [1981] 1 All ER 843, referred to above, 2.5.3). The map should also be taken from the latest Ordnance Survey edition and the prior consent of the Controller of HM Stationery Office needs to be obtained for its use.

3.9.2   Plans and diagrams

A plan or diagram ought to be considered for inclusion in a legal document which deals with technical matters. For example, architects' drawings may be included in a schedule to a building contract so as to leave no doubt between the parties as to what is to be constructed and the specifications which must be met.

Similarly, a plan or diagram for the construction of a door, fireplace or item of furniture could usefully be appended to a contract commissioning this type of work. It will have the advantage of conveying to the party who is to undertake the work the nature of the task she must complete, and the party who commissioned the work can ensure that she does not receive something different from that which she intended. Plans and diagrams may be made clearer by the use of colour, and with the advent of colour photocopiers this facility should be considered if it will assist clarity.

CHAPTER

4 Definitions

I hate definitions.

Benjamin Disraeli
Vivian Grey

4.1 Introduction

In many legal documents, particularly those of some length and complexity, a list of definitions of words and terms used in the document may be found either at the beginning or at the end of the document. It is not essential that a legal document should contain definitions of words and terms, and in simple documents there may be no need to include them. However, a word or term should be defined if it is used frequently and is intended to have a specific meaning in the document which would not ordinarily be ascribed to it. For example, in a trust deed governing a settlement for the children of a settlor's second marriage, 'children' might be defined to exclude the children of the settlor's first marriage, who would be the settlor's children under the ordinary dictionary meaning of that word.

Definitions may also be used to avoid constant repetition of a cumbersome term or reference which arises in many places throughout a document. For example, in a share sale agreement, frequent references to provisions in the Income and Corporation Taxes Act 1988 would require citation of the full title of this Act, and this could be avoided by indicating in the definitions that 'the Taxes Act' or 'the 1988 Act' refers to it.

There are many different ways, apart from the instances already mentioned, in which definitions may be used and these are referred to in this chapter. In all cases, the main purpose will be either to avoid ambiguity which might otherwise arise if the word or term was not defined, or to avoid unnecessary repetition.

4.2   Rules for the use of definitions

In using definitions in a document, the following rules should be observed.

4.2.1   Definitions should be placed at the beginning or end of the document

If definitions are needed, common sense dictates that they should be placed in the document where they can be found easily by anyone who needs to read it. It is usual to place them at the beginning or, as in statutes, at the end. Whether they are at the beginning or end is a matter of choice. However, in most commercial documents, definitions are placed at the beginning, because they will need to be referred to in reading the document and are less likely to be overlooked by the reader if placed there.

4.2.2   List definitions in alphabetical order

The list of definitions should be in alphabetical order to facilitate reference. This will be particularly important in a document with a long list of definitions, in order to avoid wasting the reader's time going through all the definitions to discover whether a word or term has a specific meaning in the document. If dates are used to begin definitions as, for example, where an Act of Parliament is referred to as 'the 1925 Act' or 'the 1990 Act', these should be placed at either the beginning or the end of the list of definitions. In addition, words and terms chosen as definitions should be of a type which are commonly used in the context. For example, in a pension scheme trust deed, a definition of 'Final Remuneration' or 'Final Salary' might be expected. and the use of an unusual term in this context, such as 'Ultimate Consideration', would not be helpful. The definitions might be numbered consecutively, if it is felt that this would improve the document.

4.2.3   First letter of definitions in capitals

Words and terms used as definitions in a document must be distinguished from ordinary words and terms which are not so used, particularly those which are the same as the definitions. This distinction is normally made by commencing all words and terms which are used as definitions with a capital letter. For example, if a particular company was defined throughout an agreement as 'the company', it should be cited as 'the Company' to distinguish it from other companies, which may be referred to as 'the company'. Similarly, in a trust deed, the trustees of the trust may be defined in order to avoid confusion with the trustees of some other trust which is referred to in the deed, and the trustees of the trust will be defined as 'the Trustees' and referred to as such throughout the deed. If a definition consists of several words, then each word should begin with a capital. For example, if the term 'final repayment date' is defined in a loan agreement, it should be referred to as 'Final Repayment Date'. Definitions may also be underlined wherever they are used if it is felt this would help identify them in the document.

4.2.4   Redundant definitions

A word or term used in a document does not need to be defined if it is unambiguous in the context in which it is used. A definition for such a word or term is redundant as it serves no purpose. Indeed, the addition of a useless definition could cause trouble as it may lead the reader of the document to suppose that it has some purpose and waste time fruitlessly in searching for this. Although this may seem a statement of the obvious, redundant definitions are found in surprisingly large numbers. Often this is because a definition is not struck out of a precedent when it is redundant, or because a document is an amalgam of material from several sources and care has not been taken to check the relevance of all the definitions used. Whether a definition is redundant will be apparent from the document, and the following are examples of definitions which serve no purpose:

'Deed' means a legal document.

'Agreement' means a contract.

4.2.5 Once-only definitions

There is no point in using a definition as a label to refer to a company or a person referred to only once or twice in a document. Instead, they should be referred to by their proper names. However, some words or terms may need to be defined, even if they are used only once or twice, if it is intended that they should have a meaning either wider or narrower than that which they would ordinarily have or they are necessary to give guidance on an important matter. For example, the trust deed of a company pension scheme will normally contain discretionary trusts for the payment of a cash lump sum on the death of a member in employment. The class of beneficiaries to whom this may be paid will usually be defined by the trust deed as the 'Discretionary Beneficiaries', and this definition may only be mentioned once or twice. The definition will, nevertheless, be necessary, since the trustees need a specific reference to ensure that they are exercising their discretion in favour of an object of their power.

4.2.6 Unnecessary definitions

The use of ambiguous words or terms which will, in turn, require definitions to resolve their inherent ambiguity should be avoided. Unambiguous terms should be used wherever possible to cut down the need for unnecessary definitions. For example, if a particular date is referred to in a document, it should not be referred to as 'the relevant date' and then defined as, say, '12 January 2001', when it would be possible to refer to 12 January 2001 everywhere the term 'the relevant date' was used. Indeed, 'the relevant date' as a term tends to detract from the clarity of the document. Similarly, in a will it would be inappropriate to set out a testator's wish to leave all his property to X by drafting it as 'all my Money to X' and then defining 'Money' as being all the testator's property. There is no need for a definition in this case if the gift is drafted as 'all my property to X'.

4.3   Methods of defining words and terms

Definitions can be put to a number of different uses in a document. Consider the following uses.

4.3.1   Definitions which restrict the meaning of a word

The ordinary dictionary meaning of a word may be of wider import than is required in the context of a document, but a suitable alternative which conveys the narrower intended meaning may not exist. In these circumstances, the word may be defined so that it is restricted to the narrower meaning for the purposes of the document. This is done by indicating in the definition what is *excluded* from the meaning of the word as used in its defined sense. For example, if a testator wants to establish a trust in his will for a large number, but not all, of his numerous nieces, the use of the term 'nieces' without definition would be inappropriate, as it would include nieces who are not intended to be beneficiaries. Reference to individual nieces by name everywhere in the document would be unduly cumbersome, and it is unlikely that a suitable alternative could be found which would accurately and concisely define the class intended. Thus, one course is to define 'nieces' in a way which excludes nieces who are not the objects of the trust. There are a number of ways in which this might be done, but perhaps the most obvious is to list all nieces intended as beneficiaries in the definition. Since the word, as a definition, is limited to only some of the objects which would ordinarily fall within its meaning, those objects not included are excluded by implication.

The following examples also illustrate how a definition can be restricted in its meaning by excluding, by implication, what is not expressly included:

'Company' means a public company as defined by the Companies Acts.

'Notice' means a notice in writing.

In the first example, private companies, at least, are excluded; in the second example, any form of notice other than the one in writing is excluded.

A definition may also restrict the meaning of a word to a particular time or area, as in the following illustrations:

'Conveyance' means a conveyance made after 30 June 2000.

'Employee' means an employee whose employment with the employer commenced after 1 January 2000.

'Land' means land in England and Wales.

4.3.2   Definitions which extend the ordinary meaning of a word

The ordinary meaning of a word may be extended by a definition so that it includes something which is not within its ordinary material meaning, but is not such as to give it an extraordinary meaning. This technique is normally used when there is no suitable alternative word which would accurately include both what the defined word ordinarily includes *plus* its extended meaning as defined. For example, the following definitions include things which would not normally fall within them:

'Business' includes any profession or trade.

'Cash' includes money in any form.

'Wife' includes a former wife.

4.3.3   Definitions which give words an extraordinary meaning

Sometimes, a definition may be given to a word or term which could not be attributed to it in ordinary usage. It is unwise to give a definition an extraordinary meaning, as a reader would not expect the word or term to bear that meaning and may find it difficult to keep this meaning in mind. The result may be confusion or mistakes by the reader. The following definitions illustrate an unnatural meaning:

'Motor Vehicle' includes a bicycle or any horse drawn carriage.

'House' includes a caravan.

Since neither a bicycle nor a horse drawn carriage has a motor engine, the definition 'Motor Vehicle' is unnaturally wide. A caravan would not be ordinarily described as a house, so the definition of 'House' is unnatural and could be replaced by a definition which is more suitable to the context, such as 'Dwelling'.

Definitions of this type are not wholly unacceptable, but they require care in their use. There may be occasions where their use is unavoidable because a suitable alternative could be found for the context of the document.

4.3.4   Definitions which label long terms

Sometimes, an individual, company or unincorporated body with a long name, or a statute with a long title, needs to be referred to in a document. In either case, the constant repetition of the long name or title will add to the length of the document and detract from its clarity in those places where it needs to be mentioned. This can be avoided by using a label to refer to the name or title which is either a single word or appropriate initials, as in the following examples:

'Taxes Act' means the Income and Corporation Taxes Act 1988.

'Company' means the Universal General Manufacturing and Trading Company Limited.

'IBC' means International Brick Company plc.

In addition to labelling an inconveniently long term, a labelling definition can also be used to refer to a class of persons or a collection of things which could not be easily referred to individually in the document, as the following example illustrates:

'Shareholders' means persons listed for the time being as shareholders in the Company's register of shareholders.

4.3.5   Definitions which substitute or delegate

A definition may indicate not only to whom or to what it refers, but
then go on to indicate that other persons or things may fall within
the definition by way of substitution or delegation. In this sense, the
definition may avoid the need for provisions in the document on
substitution or delegation. For example, a business loan agreement
may define 'Auditors' as follows:

> 'Auditors' means Brown and Co or such other firm of chartered
> accountants of internationally recognised standing as are
> appointed auditors of the Borrower and its Subsidiaries.

Definitions which substitute or delegate can add flexibility to a
document and avoid the need for amendments in future. For
example, it is common in trust deeds to define the 'Trustees' as the
trustees for the time being, rather than as named individuals who
hold the office of trustee.

4.3.6   Definitions which clarify

Sometimes, a word or term used in a document may leave doubt in
the mind of the reader as to exactly what is or is not intended to be
included in it. This may be due to the fact that the dictionary
meaning of the word is not clear, and it has not been possible to
find a more precise and usable alternative. A definition of that word
or term may be included in the document so as to eliminate doubt.
Such definitions are, in essence, 'for the avoidance of doubt'. Thus,
for example, it may be necessary to define 'month' in an agreement
or lease as referring to 'calendar month' or to define 'stocks and
shares' in a deed as including all forms of investment dealt with on
the stock exchange.

4.4   Common problems in drafting definitions

In drafting definitions, it is vital to ensure that they will work in the
context in which they are used and that their content (that is, what
is included in or omitted from them) will not cause difficulties. Poorly

drafted definitions often indicate that the lawyer may not have fully understood the subject matter with which he is dealing or that he has used a precedent, but has failed to amend its definitions to meet the requirements of his task. Unless a definition is considered in the context in which it is used, its inadequacies may not become apparent until the document has been executed and when it is, normally, too late to take action to deal with the problem. The following problems can arise in relation to definitions.

4.4.1 Omissions

A definition may, when considered together with other definitions in a document, or in the context in which it is used, reveal that it has failed to deal with a particular matter.

Omissions can sometimes occur when the rights of individuals are defined by reference to a particular date or age or qualification. For example, the rules of a members' club may provide for different privileges for two classes of members, defined as follows:

'Old Members' means members who joined before 31 December 2000.

'New Members' means members who joined after 1 January 2001.

When these definitions are considered together it is apparent that members who joined on 31 December 2000 or on 1 January 2001 are neither Old Members nor New Members. The omission could have been avoided by inserting the words 'on or' after 'joined' in each definition.

4.4.2 Overlaps between definitions

Definitions can cause confusion if they overlap. An overlap may only be apparent when the definitions are read together or when they are applied in a particular context, as the following example illustrates:

'Excluded Person' means a person who was born after 1 January 1990.

'Included Person' means a person who was born before 31 December 1991.

As these definitions are likely to be separated in an alphabetical list of definitions by other definitions, they must be considered together to ensure that they do not overlap. The overlap in the example above is likely to have arisen from a failure to transpose the year correctly in one of the definitions. A reader of the document may not have sufficient background knowledge to determine which definition is correct and if the error is discovered many years later there may be no evidence at that time to resolve the problem.

4.4.3 Multiple definitions for one meaning

Confusion can also arise where parts of different precedents are put together to form one document, with the result that two definitions are used for the same thing. Thus, for example, in a contract cobbled together from different sources, one source might refer to the 'Employer' and the other source to the 'Company'. If 'Employer' is struck out of the definitions section, but is nevertheless used as a definition in parts of the document, the reader will have to decide whether 'Employer' should be read as 'Company'. This may not cause any difficulty so long as the 'Employer' and the 'Company' are the same person or legal entity, but if, at a later date, they are no longer the same, this could lead to problems. For example, if a clause in the document states 'the Employer shall pay ...', and the Company is defined, but the Employer is not, it may be unclear who must pay.

4.4.4 Loaded definitions

Sometimes, definitions are loaded with material which should properly appear elsewhere in the document. The object of a definition is to define, and not to set out rights, duties, powers, or privileges. These should be set out in the clauses in the document, since the reader would not expect to find such matters dealt with in the definitions and may overlook them or find it difficult to retain the additional information in mind when reading the document. For example, the following definition is taken from an Inland Revenue document which limits the benefits payable from an exempt approved pension scheme:

> 'Class C Member' means any Member who joined the scheme before 17 March 1987 provided that the Member may elect, at any time, before the Relevant Date to be deemed to have become a Class A Member on 1 June 1989.

The right of election might be better placed in a substantive provision in the document.

Definitions may also be loaded, not because they refer to specific duties, powers and privileges, but because they contain too much material by way of definition. In such instances, consideration should be given to whether some or all of the material concerned should be set out in a clause in the document.

4.4.5   Provisos in definitions

Provisos in definitions make exceptions or qualifications to that definition. Provisos should be avoided for two reasons. First, the addition of provisos will make it more difficult for the reader to grasp the concepts which are defined and probably require him to read and re-read the definition to try to work out what it is intended to embody. Secondly, the addition of provisos making exceptions or qualifications to a definition is likely to create difficulty for the reader in applying the concept embodied in the definition in those parts of the document where it is used. He will probably find it necessary to refer back constantly to the definition. This is not only irritating, but may indicate that little care was exercised in drafting the definition in the first place. In many cases, the need for a proviso in a definition can be eliminated if the trouble is taken to redraft the definition. The use of provisos is explored further below, Chapter 6.

CHAPTER

5

Drafting Language

If language is not correct, then what is said is not what is meant; if what is said is not what is meant, then what ought to be done remains undone.

Confucius (551–479 BC)

5.1   Introduction

This chapter and following two chapters is primarily concerned with the words used to communicate the concepts in a legal document and the structure of legal sentences. In this chapter and Chapter 6, consideration is given to some matters which should be borne in mind when choosing words to compose a document and its sentence structure. In Chapter 7, the use of certain words and expressions which can give rise to difficulties in drafting is examined.

5.2   Drafting as communication

5.2.1   General

Successful oral communication occurs when the hearer's understanding is identical to the speaker's meaning. Similarly, successful legal drafting depends upon the lawyer choosing words to express the concepts to be communicated so that the reader's understanding will be identical to the lawyer's meaning. In many cases, the lawyer may need to go further and ensure that the reader's understanding cannot be different from his meaning. This will be necessary if the rights and obligations set out in a document confer valuable benefits or impose financial burdens, or where a party would gladly welcome the opportunity to avoid an obligation imposed upon him by the document. In *Re Castioni* [1891] 1

QB 149, Stephen J remarked on the importance of the latter point in the context of legislative drafting. He said:

> I think that my late friend, Mr Mill, made a mistake upon the subject, probably because he was not accustomed to use language with that degree of precision which is essential to anyone who has ever had, as I have on many occasions, to draft Acts of Parliament, which, although they may be easy to understand, people continually try to misunderstand, and which, therefore, it is not enough to attain to a degree which a person reading in good faith can understand, but it is necessary to attain, if possible, to a degree of precision which a person reading in bad faith cannot misunderstand. It is all the better if he cannot pretend to misunderstand it.

5.2.2   Intention drawn from words used

Drafting, like any written communication, does not have any of the props which often support oral communication and assist the hearer in determining the speaker's intentions. The props in oral communication include facial expressions, gestures and intonation. These, plus the fact that the speaker and the hearer may be known to each other, assist oral communication. In drafting, the lawyer must rely on words alone to convey his intentions in a document. To ensure that the intention is conveyed to the reader, simple words should be used in accordance with their ordinary natural meaning. This is because it is a fundamental rule of construction that the intention behind a legal document must be deduced from the words used, as has been repeatedly pointed out in the cases:

> ... in construing instruments you must have regard, not to the presumed intention of the parties, but to the meaning of the words which they have used.
>
> *Re Meredith* (1989) 11 Ch D 731, p 739, *per* Brett LJ

> One must consider the meaning of the words used, not what one may guess to be the intention of the parties.
>
> *Smith v Lucas* (1881) 18 Ch D 531, p 542, *per* Jessel MR

... what a man intends and the expression of his intention are two different things. He is bound and those who take after him are bound by his expressed intention. If that expressed intention is unfortunately different from what he really desires, so much the worse for those who wish the actual intention to prevail.

Simpson v Foxon [1907] P 54, p 57, *per* Sir Gorrell Barnes P

5.2.3   Use words in their ordinary meaning

It is a long established rule of construction that words used in a legal document will, unless the context shows otherwise, be construed according to their ordinary and natural meaning. As Jessel MR said in *Re Levy* (1881) 17 Ch D 746, p 751:

... the grammatical and ordinary sense of the words is to be adhered to, unless that would lead to some absurdity, or some repugnance or inconsistency with the rest of the instrument, in which case the grammatical or ordinary sense of the words may be modified, so as to avoid that absurdity and inconsistency and no further.

The use of words in accordance with their ordinary and natural meaning should ensure that the concepts behind a document are accurately conveyed to the reader. For example, if a will contains a bequest of 'all my stocks and shares', the ordinary natural meaning of these words confines them to the stocks and shares in limited companies and, therefore, would not include government securities (see *Re Everett* [1944] Ch 176). Similarly, a bequest of 'all my cars' would not include vans or lorries. Sometimes, it may be difficult to determine the ordinary and natural meaning of words. This meaning is not always the dictionary meaning. It may be the popular meaning at the time that the document was drafted, or a particular meaning which the parties attribute to the words.

Decided cases are of little value as a guide to how particular words might be construed if used in a document. In *Tophams Ltd v Sefton* [1967] AC 50, the defendant covenanted not to 'cause or permit' the Aintree racecourse to be used other than for horse racing. The defendant agreed to sell the land to a property developer whom it knew would use the land for housebuilding. It was alleged that the defendant was in breach of covenant. Many cases were cited to the House of Lords in which the words 'permit' had been construed by the court. Lord Wilberforce found these unhelpful. He said:

> ... the use of precedents to attribute to plain English words a meaning derived from the use of those words in other documents is always of doubtful value and the inutility of this procedure is exemplified here. The cases in fact give no more than illustrations of the use of the word 'permit' in certain isolated factual situations, and illustration is something less than we need.

The cases show that the ordinary and natural meaning of words can shift and that the context in which they are used is an important controlling factor in deciding their meaning. For example, a trust deed will usually contain an express power directing the trustees to 'invest' the trust funds. The *Shorter Oxford English Dictionary* states that 'invest' means 'to employ money in the purchase of anything from which interest or profit is expected'. This includes earned income and capital appreciation. In *Re Power* [1947] Ch 572, an express clause directing the trustees to 'invest' the trust fund was confined to investments producing income, because the trust provided for the income to be paid to a life tenant and the capital to remaindermen; capital appreciation alone would not give the life tenant an income.

5.3   Vagueness

5.3.1   Problems with vague words

Vagueness arises from the use of words which do not have any specific boundaries and, therefore, give a choice as to their degree or extent. For example, if a customer orders a red car from a motor dealer, it is clear that a blue car would not satisfy the contract description. But, an order for a blue car does not specify the shade of blue the customer has in mind. Delivery of a navy blue car is within the bounds of what was ordered, but it may be rejected. The dealer may wish to avoid the risk of the customer rejecting the car by requiring him to specify the shade of blue required.

As a general rule, vague words should be avoided in legal drafting as they are likely to lead to disputes and in extreme cases may lead to such a degree of uncertainty that a provision in which they are used is treated as void. Thus, in a contract which allows one party to receive additional payments for 'sundries' or 'miscellaneous expenses', there is a risk disputes may arise because the parties differ as to what the terms include. If the parties insist on using such vague terms, they should at least be defined for the purposes of the document so that it is clear what is included or excluded from their ambit in the context in which they are used. For example, if a contract of employment entitles an employee to additional payments for 'emergency work' or work done outside 'normal hours', these vague terms should be defined.

One route by which vague terms can enter a legal document is by the use of euphemisms where it is felt clear words would have alarming or unpleasant connotations. Lord Merriman P criticised the use of euphemisms in an unreported divorce case in 1959. He said:

> It is a pity that plain English is not used about these matters in divorce proceedings. When I say plain English I mean that, so far as I know, ever since the tablets of stone were translated into English in the English version of the Bible, 'adultery' has been the word, not 'misconduct' or 'intimacy' or any other paraphrase of it.

Thus, for example, references to a wife as a 'partner', 'friend', or 'associate' should be avoided, as should references to 'deceased' as 'departed' or 'asleep'.

5.3.2 Vague words may lead to uncertainty

Some words are so imprecise in their meaning that it is difficult, if not impossible, to decide what does or does not fall within their boundaries, with the result that a provision in which they are used may be void for uncertainty. Dispositions under wills and trusts provide many examples of the use of vague words to define a class of beneficiaries. In *Re Gulbenkian's Settlement Trusts* [1970]

AC 508, Lord Upjohn made the following observations on the use of vague words to define a class of beneficiaries who are to benefit equally under a trust:

> ... suppose the donor directs that a fund is to be divided equally between 'my old friends', then unless there is some admissible evidence that the donor has given some special 'dictionary' meaning to that phrase which enables the trustee to identify the class with sufficient certainty, it is plainly bad as being too uncertain. Suppose that there appeared before the trustees (or the court) two or three individuals who plainly satisfied the test of being among 'my old friends', the trustees could not consistently with the donor's intentions accept them as claiming the whole or any defined part of the fund.

The use of terms such as 'residents', 'relatives', 'dependants', 'friends', and 'persons having a moral claim upon X' have all resulted in difficulties, particularly in the distribution of funds under non-discretionary trusts. However, it is not only in the area of wills and trusts that vague words can lead to uncertainty, so that a provision fails. In *National Trust v Midlands Electricity Board* [1952] Ch 380, Vaisey J was asked to decide whether the erection of electricity poles was in breach of a covenant which stated:

> No act or thing shall be done or placed or permitted to remain upon the land which shall injure prejudice affect or destroy the natural aspect and condition of the land ...

He concluded that the words used in the covenant were so vague as to be void for uncertainty.

5.3.3   Avoiding uncertainty where vague words are used

Circumstances can arise where the use of vague words cannot be avoided because, for example, a client insists upon them. One method by which potential uncertainty arising from their use can be avoided is, as already indicated, by giving the words a defined meaning. Another method is by giving a named individual power to determine the scope of the words. In *Re Tuck's Settlement Trusts* [1978] 1 All ER 1047, the income of a settlement was payable to a beneficiary only if he was of the 'Jewish faith' and married to a woman of the 'Jewish blood'. These terms were not void for uncertainty in this case, but Lord Denning MR suggested that, even if they had been, the trust would still have been valid because the settlor decided that any dispute or doubt on these matters was to be decided by the chief rabbi. He said:

> If two contracting parties can agree to leave a doubt or difficulty to be decided by a third person, I see no reason why a testator or settlor should not leave the decision to his trustees or a third party. He does not thereby oust the jurisdiction of the court.

Thus, in *National Trust v Midlands Electricity Board* [1952] Ch 380, the covenant would have been valid if the words 'in the opinion of the covenantee' had been inserted between 'shall' and 'injure', so that it read:

> No act or thing shall be done or placed or permitted to remain upon the land which shall, in the opinion of the covenantee, injure prejudice affect or destroy the natural aspect and condition of the land ...

5.3.4 Circumstances where vague words are appropriate

Although vague words can cause difficulties, they can also serve a useful purpose in legal drafting, especially where the terms of a document are a matter of negotiation between two or more parties. In these cases, they may enable the parties to reach a compromise so that a transaction may proceed. As Lord Wilberforce remarked in *Prenn v Simmonds* [1971] 3 All ER 237:

> ... the words used may and often do represent a formula which means different things to each side, yet may be accepted because it is the only way to get agreement in the hope that disputes will not arise.

For example, the parties to a building contract may be unable to agree the date by which the builder is to complete the work. This might be compromised by stipulating that it is to be done in 'a reasonable time' and, if appropriate, by stipulating an upper limit on the date by which it must be completed, such as 'a reasonable time but not later than 1 December 2001'. Similarly, a party to an agreement who is required to obtain consent or permission (such as planning permission for building work) from a third party may not wish to give an absolute undertaking in this respect. Instead, he may be prepared only to take 'reasonable steps' or to use 'reasonable endeavours' to obtain such permission.

5.4   Ambiguity

5.4.1   Problems with ambiguity

Ambiguity occurs where words are capable of bearing two or more meanings in the circumstances in which they are used. It may arise in a legal document in three ways. First, because a word which has two or more meanings is used in circumstances where it is unclear which of those meanings is intended. This is semantic ambiguity. Secondly, the manner in which the words chosen to convey a legal concept are arranged may be such that they are capable of having more than one meaning. This is known as syntactic ambiguity. Thirdly, clear words in a document may, when other facts are taken into account, show that there is a conflict in the application of those words to the circumstances in which they are intended to operate. This is contextual ambiguity.

The dangers of ambiguity arising in a legal document can be reduced by following the drafting rules mentioned in this chapter and in Chapters 6 and 7 and, in particular, by using short and simple words (see below, 5.5), consistency in references (see below, 5.6), the proper composition of clauses (see below, 6.2) and the use of punctuation (see below, 6.4). It may also be prevented by reading through a draft critically and viewing it from all angles so as to ensure that it can be interpreted in only one way.

5.4.2   Semantic ambiguity

Many words in the English language have several meanings: for example, 'bar' can mean to exclude, a tavern, a line, or to close; 'light' can mean lamp, fire, not heavy, truth, or funny; and 'pipe' can mean tube, flute, or tobacco pipe. Semantic ambiguity does not simply arise from the use of a word which has several meanings, but only if that word is used in a context in which it is unclear which meaning is intended. As Lord Reid said in *Kirkness (Inspector of Taxes) v Hudson* [1955] AC 696, p 735:

> A provision is not ambiguous merely because it contains a word which in different contexts is capable of different meanings. It would be hard to find anywhere a sentence of any length which does not contain such a word. A provision is, in my judgment, ambiguous only if it contains a word or phrase which in that particular context is capable of bearing more than one meaning.

If a word with several meanings is used in a legal document, it is likely that, in most instances, the context will indicate which meaning it is to bear. For example, if a loan agreement refers to 'a bank', it is likely that this means a financial institution rather than the ground at the side of a river or a slope. If there is a danger that semantic ambiguity may arise from the use of a word which has several meanings, a synonym should be used to ensure that the appropriate meaning is conveyed. In *Perrin v Morgan* [1943] AC 399, a testatrix left 'all the moneys I die possessed of' to her nephews and nieces. 'Moneys' could be construed as either cash and funds deposited in the bank or all the testatrix's wealth. The House of Lords held that the latter meaning applied, on the basis that 'moneys' was used in its popular sense, rather than in its strict legal sense. The use of an alternative to 'moneys' would have been desirable, and terms such as 'all my property' or 'all my estate' would have avoided the need for the court to construe the will.

5.4.3   Syntactic ambiguity

The manner in which words are arranged in a sentence may result in that sentence being open to two or more interpretations. William Cobbett wrote of this in 1818: '... of all the faults in writing, the wrong placing of words is one of the most common, and perhaps it leads to the greatest number of misconceptions.' An illustration of this, which has appeared in many books on grammar, is 'piano for sale by a lady going abroad in an oak case with carved legs'.

In legal drafting, syntactic ambiguity may arise because words which are intended to restrict, limit or make more exact the meaning of other words are misplaced in a sentence. It is crucial that it is clear which words within a sentence qualify the meaning of other words within the same sentence. For example, in a gift for 'religious bodies or schools', 'religious' could be treated as referring to 'bodies' or as qualifying both 'bodies' and 'schools', so that only religious schools could benefit. Similarly, in a gift for 'charitable, benevolent or public objects in the parish of Faringdon', the words 'in the parish of Faringdon' could be interpreted as limiting all the objects to the parish of Faringdon, or as qualifying only 'public objects'.

5.4.4   Contextual ambiguity

The words used in a legal document may, in themselves, be perfectly clear on the face of the document, but when further facts are disclosed ambiguity appears. This is contextual ambiguity, and it may arise in three main ways.

First, contextual ambiguity may arise when words are applied to the circumstances in which they are intended to operate. For example, if a testator directs in his will 'all my estate to my son', the disposition is unambiguous on reading the will. But, if the testator has three sons, there is ambiguity, as the disposition could refer to any one of the sons. Rules of construction may be able to resolve this ambiguity, but if the disposition was drafted with greater precision, or steps taken to find out if the testator had more than one son, the trouble and expense this would involve would be avoided.

Secondly, contextual ambiguity may result from the excessive use of pronouns such as 'he', 'she', 'him', 'her', 'it' or 'they' in the place of proper names, with the result that it is unclear which of two or more persons or things they refer to. If a clause refers to one individual or thing, the use of a pronoun may avoid unnecessary repetition of a name, especially if it is long, without any possibility of ambiguity. For example, if a lease states: 'The tenant covenants with the landlord that he will not alter or add to the buildings on the property except with the consent of the landlord,' it is clear that 'he' refers to the tenant rather than the landlord. If a pronoun could refer to two or more parties to a document, it should not be used; for example, if a lease states: 'The landlord will lease Blackacre to the tenant and he will pay £10,000 to him,' it is not clear who is meant by 'he' and 'him' in this provision. If the £10,000 is payable by the tenant in consideration of the grant of the lease to him, express reference should be made to him, for example: 'Upon payment by the tenant of £10,000 to the landlord, the landlord will lease Blackacre to the tenant.'

Thirdly, contextual ambiguity may occur where different provisions in a document purport to deal with the same thing in different ways. If clause 1 of a will devises Redacre to X and clause 18 of the same will devises Redacre to Y, there is a conflict. In this instance, a rule of construction that the latter provision is to prevail may resolve the conflict. However, it is unsatisfactory that the identity of the beneficiary should depend on a rule of construction, and the problem ought to be avoided by reading through the will to ensure it does not contain any internal conflicts.

5.5   Use short and simple words

5.5.1   General

Obscure words and expressions are sometimes found in legal documents which, although not necessarily archaic, could be replaced by much simpler words and expressions which would improve clarity without altering meaning. Since the document is intended to communicate to the reader in the clearest possible terms, the words and expressions chosen should not leave any doubt as to their intended meaning. A document expressed in unduly complicated language merely exhibits a lack of consideration for the reader.

5.5.2   Achieving simple language

Fowler and Fowler's *The King's English* contains some positive advice on grammar and style and on the use of words. It advises:

• Prefer the familiar word to the far-fetched.

• Prefer the concrete word to the abstract.

• Prefer the single word to the circumlocution.

• Prefer the short word to the long.

• Prefer the Saxon word to the Romance.

These rules were given by Fowler in order of merit and he pointed out that 'the last is also the least'. The fourth and fifth rules have attracted some disagreement. In drafting, the first three rules are important, since they concern communication and precision. Fowler acknowledged that these rules overlapped and by way of example referred to 'in the contemplated eventuality', which is 'at once the far-fetched, the abstract, the periphrastic, the long and the Romance for "if so"'. He also accepted that these were general rules and could be subject to exception in certain kinds of composition. However, in legal drafting, there are unlikely to be many instances where they are subject to exceptions.

5.5.3   Familiar words

Where there is a choice between two words, and one is short and familiar and the other is long and unusual, the former should be preferred. For example, an agreement for the sale of a washing machine would be unduly pompous if it referred to the 'vendor' and the 'purchaser'. The terms 'seller' and 'buyer' would be more suitable. Latin terms should be avoided where possible. For example, *mutatis mutandis* or *inter alia* could be replaced by 'the necessary changes being made' and 'amongst other things'. The following list (which is not exhaustive) sets out in the left hand column further examples of unfamiliar words which could be replaced by the familiar words in the right hand column:

accorded	given
afforded	given
cease	stop
consequence	result
deemed	considered
effectuate	carry out
evince	show
expend	spend
expiration	end
feasible	possible
forthwith	immediately
implement	carry out
indenture	deed
indicate	show
institute	begin
lessee	tenant
lessor	landlord

per centum . . . . per cent

portion . . . . part

possess . . . . have

procure . . . . obtain

purchaser . . . . buyer

remainder . . . . rest

retain . . . . keep

specified . . . . named

suffer . . . . permit

vendor . . . . seller

whereabouts . . . . location

with reference to . . . . . for

5.5.4   Concrete words

Concrete words and expressions should be used in preference to abstract words and expressions. As Fowler remarked:

> A writer uses abstract words because his thoughts are cloudy; the habit of using them clouds his thoughts still further; he may end up by concealing his meaning not only from his readers, but also from himself.

The following examples of the use of abstract expressions are cited by Gower in *The Complete Plain Words*:

> The actual date of completion of the purchase should coincide with the availability of the new facilities.

That is, 'the purchase should not be completed until the new facilities are available'.

> The availability of figures may indeed prove to be one of the obstacles in the efficiency of the whole of the proposed statistical content of the exercise.

In other words, 'lack of figures may make it difficult to produce accurate statistics'.

The abstract may creep into a legal document through the use of abstract nouns where a concrete noun could be used. The former names an attribute or a quality of a thing, whilst the latter names the thing regarded as possessing that attribute or quality. For example, if it is necessary to refer to the will of X in another legal document, this should not be in the abstract form 'a legal document executed by X on ...', as it is imprecise and could include other legal documents made by X on that date. Similarly, if a contract states 'you will provide your services on a consultancy basis', this would be clearer in concrete terms such as 'you will act as a consultant'.

5.5.5   Single words

Phrases are sometimes used in legal documents which are little more than a roundabout way of expressing something which could be stated in one word. Where a document is infested with these circumlocutions, it will be unnecessarily long. For example, it is unnecessary to say 'in the event that' when 'if' would do equally well, or 'under the provisions of' when 'under' is sufficient. The following list contains some further examples which can be avoided:

1st day of January 2001	1 January 2001
admit of	allow
all and singular	all
at the time	when
by means of	by
contiguous to	next to
covenant and agree	agree
does not operate to	does not
doth grant	grants
doth order	orders

during such time as . . . . while

each and every . . . . each (or every)

enter into a contract with . . . . contract with

falls into and becomes part of . . . becomes part of

for the duration of . . . . during

for the reason that . . . . because

in the event that . . . . if

in lieu of . . . . in place of

in order to . . . . to

in the interest of . . . . for

is able to . . . . can

is binding upon . . . . binds

it is the duty . . . . shall

it shall be lawful . . . . may

lands, tenements
and hereditaments . . . . lands

last will and testamentlast . . . . . . will

made and entered into . . . . made

mutually agree . . . . agree

now these presents . . . . this agreement

on the part of . . . . by

or, in the alternative . . . . or

party of the first part . . . . (1)

party of the second part . . . . (2)

pursuant to . . . . under

right, title and interest . . . . interest

subsequent to . . . . after

to have and to hold . . . . have

to the effect that . . . . that

under the provisions of . . . . under

until such time . . . . until

with reference to . . . . for

5.5.6 Short words

The following list (which is not exhaustive) contains words and expressions in the left hand column which are frequently used in legal documents and which could be replaced by the words and expressions in the right hand column so as to improve clarity:

1st day of January 2001 . . . . 1 January 2001

accorded . . . . given

admit of . . . . allow

afforded . . . . given

all and singular . . . . all

at the time . . . . when

by means of . . . . by

cease . . . . stop

consequence . . . . result

contiguous to . . . . next to

covenant and agree . . . . agree

deemed . . . . considered

does not operate to . . . . does not

doth grant . . . . grants

doth order . . . . orders

during such time as . . . . while

each and every .... each (or every)

effectuate .... carry out

enter into a contract with .... contract with

evince .... show

expend .... spend

expiration .... end

falls into and becomes part of ... becomes part of

feasible .... possible

for the duration of .... during

for the reason that .... because

forthwith .... immediately

implement .... carry out

in the event that .... if

in lieu of .... in place of

in order to .... to

in the interest of .... for

indenture .... deed

indicate .... show

institute .... begin

is able to .... can

is binding upon .... binds

it is the duty .... shall

it shall be lawful .... may

lands, tenements
     and hereditaments .... lands

last will and testament .... last will

lessee .... tenant

lessor .... landlord

made and entered into	made
mutually agree	agree
now these presents	this agreement
witnesseth	witnesses
on the part of	by
or, in the alternative	or
party of the first part	(1)
party of the second part	(2)
per centum	per cent
portion	part
possess	have
procure	obtain
purchaser	buyer
pursuant to	under
remainder	rest
retain	keep
right, title and interest	interest
specified	named
subsequent to	after
suffer	permit
to have and to hold	have
to the effect that	that
under the provisions of	under
until such time	until
vendor	seller
whereabouts	location
with reference to	for

5.6 Consistency

5.6.1 Consistency in references

References to persons or things must be consistent throughout a legal document. For example, if a contract refers to 'the buyer', it should not be changed to 'the purchaser' or 'Mr Smith' at a later stage in the document. The different references may be treated as signifying a change in meaning. Equally, there is no place for what is described in Fowler's *Modern English Usage* as 'elegant variation', that is, expressing oneself prettily rather than clearly. The object of a legal document is to set out rights, powers or privileges and obligations or duties with precision rather than to entertain the reader. In *Hadley v Perks* (1866) LR 1 QB 444, Blackburn J said (p 57):

> It has been a general rule for drawing legal documents from the earliest times, one which one is taught when one first becomes a pupil to a conveyancer, never to change the form of words unless you are going to change the meaning ...

5.6.2 Avoiding inconsistency

Inconsistent references to a person or thing can arise in three main ways:

(a) Two or more undefined words or terms are used to refer to the same thing.

If a trust is created under a will for the benefit of X, who is described as 'the beneficiary' at the beginning of the document, he should be referred to as such throughout the document. If he is referred to as 'the legatee' or 'the donee', there is a danger that these references may be construed as applying to someone other than X. See also the example given above, 5.6.1.

Elegant variation may also lead to the unwitting imposition of rights and obligations which are either wider or narrower than intended. For example, if a lease of a house refers to 'the house', this should not be altered to 'the premises', 'the property', 'the building' or 'the estate', because it is felt that there are too many references to 'the house'. In an appropriate context, the variation could be construed as referring to something larger or smaller than the house. Thus, if the tenant orally agreed with the landlord to keep 'the house' in repair, a provision in the lease imposing an obligation on him to keep 'the property' in repair could be much wider than he agreed and it might include the garden and outbuildings.

(b) Defined words or terms used as if undefined.

If a word or term has a defined meaning for the purposes of a legal document, it must be set out in a way which shows that it is used as defined in every place in the document where this is appropriate. For example, if 'Company' or 'Spouse' are used in a document with a defined meaning, they must be used in a way that shows that the defined meaning is intended. If this is not done, the reader may well conclude that the defined meaning is not intended. For example, under a share sale agreement under which company A agrees to sell its subsidiary, company X, to company B, company X may be defined in the agreement as 'the Company' whilst companies A and B are respectively referred to as 'the Vendor' and 'the Purchaser'. If the agreement is poorly drafted so that, on occasions, it merely refers to 'the company' when it should refer to 'the Company', the reader may well conclude that either company A or B or some other company was intended in that context.

(c) Undefined word or term used to refer to two different things.

A word or term must not be used with two different meanings in the same document, since this is likely to lead to confusion. For example, if a trust is established under a will in the form of 'to A for life remainder to B absolutely', references to A and B should be either by name or by different terms. It would be inappropriate to refer to both of them as 'the beneficiary' in provisions in the will other than those setting out the trusts.

5.7   Technical legal terms

5.7.1   General considerations

There are few, if any, areas of law that do not possess technical legal words or terms which are well understood by lawyers familiar with that area of law. Sometimes, these words or terms may be known to non-lawyers because they are in general use. For example, most non-lawyers are likely to understand technical legal words such as 'lease', 'landlord', 'tenant', 'contract' or 'will'. However, the vast majority of technical legal words and terms will not be properly understood by non-lawyers, for example, words and terms such as 'deed poll', 'intestate', 'equitable interest' or 'bailment'.

The use of technical legal words and terms is sometimes criticised as legal jargon or legalese. As is indicated below, 5.8, there is justification for this criticism where technical legal language is used to excess or where it is inappropriate. However, the use of technical legal words and terms is necessary and appropriate in some instances in order to communicate the concepts with which a legal document is concerned both accurately and effectively.

5.7.2   Construction of technical legal words and terms

If technical legal words and terms are used in a legal document, they will be construed by the court primarily as having their technical legal meaning. In *Holt v Collyer* (1881) 16 Ch D 718, Fry J said:

> In my view the principle upon which words are to be construed in instruments is very plain – where there is a popular and common word used in an instrument, that word must be construed *prima*

facie in its popular and common sense. If it is a word of a technical or legal character, it must be construed according to its technical or legal meaning ...

The rule that the court will construe technical legal words and terms according to their technical legal meaning is particularly important if a legal document has been drafted by a lawyer. In such circumstances, the court will conclude that they were used in their technical legal sense. This point was alluded to by Diplock LJ in *Sydall v Castings Ltd* [1967] 1 QB 302 in his explanation of the importance of technical legal words and terms in law. He said:

> ... lawyers ... have been compelled to evolve an English language, of which the constituent words and phrases are more precise in their meaning than they are in the language of Shakespeare or of any of the passengers on the Clapham omnibus this morning. These words and phrases to which a more precise meaning is so ascribed are called by lawyers 'terms of art', but are in popular parlance known as 'legal jargon'. We lawyers must not allow this denigratory description to obscure the social justification for the use of 'terms of art' in legal documents. It is essential to the effective operation of the rule of law. The phrase 'legal jargon', however, does contain a reminder that non-lawyers are unfamiliar with the meanings which lawyers attach to particular 'terms of art'.

If a lawyer drafts a will which provides 'all my money to my nephews and nieces in equal shares', the term 'money' will be construed in its technical legal sense as referring to 'cash' and not in its popular sense as including all the testator's property. However, the cases show that if a non-lawyer prepares a legal document using technical legal words, they may be construed in their popular sense if there is evidence showing the popular meaning was intended. In *Perrin v Morgan* [1943] AC 399, the House of Lords accepted that a direction in a home-made will that 'all moneys I be possessed of shall be shared by my nephews and niece now living' was, on the evidence, intended to be a gift by the testatrix of all her property using 'money' in the popular sense. In contrast, in *Re Cooke* [1948] Ch 212, a gift in a home-made will of 'all my personal estate' was construed in the technical legal sense and did not include the testatrix's house. Harman J said:

> The words 'all my personal estate' are words so well known to lawyers that it must take a very strong context to make them include real estate ... In the absence of something to show that the phrase ought not to be so construed, I must suppose that she used the term 'personal estate' in its ordinary meaning as a term of art.

5.7.3   Use of technical legal words and terms

There are two main factors which influence the use of technical legal words and terms in drafting a legal document.

(a) Nature of document

The extent to which technical legal words and terms are used in a legal document will depend on its nature and purpose. If its purpose is to communicate rights and obligations to consumers, the use of technical legal words and terms should be kept to a minimum and if they are unavoidable they should, where appropriate, be explained in language the reader is likely to understand. For example, an agreement for the hire of a car or a residential tenancy agreement should avoid technical legal words and terms.

If, however, the document is intended mainly for use by other lawyers as, for example, a settlement, it may be assumed that they are aware of the legal meaning of technical legal words and terms used. Indeed, they are likely to read the technical legal words and terms as used in their technical legal sense.

If the document will be referred to mainly by non-lawyers, who have expertise in the field to which it relates, it is likely that they will understand most, if not all, the technical legal words and terms in that field so that their use would be appropriate. For example, a commercial lease is likely to be consulted by lawyers and surveyors who are likely to understand the technical legal terms used in leases.

(b) No suitable non-legal term

Technical legal words and terms have an established and precise meaning, as Diplock LJ pointed out in *Sydall v Castings Ltd* [1967] 1 QB 302 (above). They should only be replaced by non-technical terms if the latter will not result in a loss of precision, or would not result in the possibility of a different construction to that desired. If it is felt that either of these consequences might follow, technical legal words or terms should be preferred.

For example, it would be difficult to find suitable alternatives for 'goodwill', 'frustration' or '*per stirpes*' as used in the technical legal sense. In the case of '*per stirpes*', there is no suitable non-technical term available to act as a convenient substitute to indicate distribution by stocks of descent. To seek to explain the concept it embodies in alternative non-technical language would risk uncertainty. Another reason for using technical legal words and terms is because what may be perceived to be alternatives in fact have different technical legal meanings. For example, the terms 'children' and 'issue' require care in drafting a will, since the expression 'issue' is wider than 'children' and includes descendants of any degree. Thus, a lawyer who is instructed to draft a will leaving the testator's residuary estate to his 'children' in equal shares would not have fulfilled his instructions in drafting the gift as one to the testator's 'issue' in equal shares.

5.8   Archaic language

5.8.1   Avoid archaic language

Archaic language should not be used in legal documents. There is no magic in obscure words or incantations which have ceased to be employed in ordinary speech or writing. The reader may not be familiar with them, may have difficulty determining their meaning or misunderstand them. For example, an insurance policy which provides cover for the insured in the event of death by 'misadventure' may leave the insured in uncertainty as to the nature of the cover provided by the policy and result in unnecessary inquiries to the insurer. 'Misadventure' should be replaced by its modern equivalent: 'accident'. Similarly, a trust deed should not refer to '*cestui que trust*', but ought instead to refer to 'the beneficiary'.

5.8.2   Archaic meaning may differ from modern meaning

The archaic meaning and the modern meaning of a word or term may be different. If a word or term is used with the intention that it should have its archaic meaning, the court may interpret it according to its modern meaning so that it has a different meaning to that intended by the drafter. For example, if a modern legal document refers to absence 'beyond the seas' rather than absence 'abroad', the result may be unexpected. The archaic term 'beyond the seas' means beyond the four seas surrounding the British Isles, that is, the English Channel, the North Sea, the Irish Sea and the Arctic Ocean. Thus, 'beyond the seas' would include Jersey and Guernsey but 'abroad' would not (see *Rover International Ltd v Cannon Film Sales Ltd (No 2)* [1987] 3 All ER 986).

5.8.3   Archaic words to be avoided

The list below sets out some examples of archaic words often found in legal documents, which should be avoided. The list is not intended to be exhaustive:

above-mentioned

aforementioned

aforesaid

henceforward

herein

hereinafter

hereinbefore

heretofore

hereunto

herewith

notwithstanding

premises

said

thenceforth

therein

thereunto

therewith

to wit

undermentioned

unto

whatsoever

wherefore

whereof

whereon

wheresoever

witnesseth

5.9   Antiquated introductions

Antiquated introductions to the contents of various sections of legal documents should be avoided. Sometimes documents which are otherwise expressed in modern language are peppered with antiquated introductions which are usually made prominent in the document by the use of capitals. These introductions do not contain any magic and should be replaced by modern terminology. The following are examples of some of the antiquated introductions still in common use.

- 'Now these presents witnesseth that ...'

  This sentence is often used to introduce the operative part of an agreement or a deed. It would be better if expressed in each case as:

  > This agreement witnesses that ...

  > This deed witnesses that ...

- 'It is hereby declared that ...'

  This sentence is in common use, as in:

  > It is hereby expressly declared and agreed that ...

  Both of these phrases could be redrafted as:

  > It is declared that ...

  > It is declared and agreed that ...

It may be that the words following indicate that these phrases could be dispensed with altogether.

- 'In witness whereof the parties hereunto have set their hands to these presents as a deed on the day month and year hereinbefore mentioned ...'

  This sentence is often used, as in the following:

  > In witness whereof the parties have executed these presents as a deed ...

  These incantations may be revised to:

  > Executed as a deed on ...

  Or:

  > Signed and delivered as a deed on ...

  Or:

  > The parties have signed this document as a deed on ...

- 'This is the last will and testament of ...'

  This sentence could be replaced by:

  > This is the will of ...

- 'The parties hereunto mutually covenant, declare and agree ...'

  This sentence could be simplified to:

  > The parties agree ...

5.10 Synonyms

5.10.1 Avoid synonyms

Synonyms are words that have similar meanings, so that one can be substituted for the other without affecting the meaning of a sentence or clause. Legal documents and, in particular, those drafted in the traditional drafting style, are often padded out with strings of synonyms which do not add to the meaning of the document and, if anything, only serve to obscure it. Sometimes, two, three or even four words, all with similar meanings, are used to express a concept where one would do. For example, a clause in an agreement dealing with disputes which may arise between the parties may state that the decision of a named arbitrator shall be 'final and conclusive' and that 'all costs, charges and expenses' shall be met by a named party. If the arbitrator's decision is 'final', it cannot be made more so by adding that it shall be 'conclusive'. Either 'final' or 'conclusive' would have been sufficient. Similarly, the liabilities of the payor and the rights of the payee in respect of 'costs' are not altered by the addition of 'charges and expenses'.

5.10.2 Reasons why synonyms are used

Synonyms may creep into a legal document in three main ways:

(a) To ensure that important matters are included. In drafting an important provision, comprehensive words may be necessary to ensure that every eventuality that may arise will be covered. If one word is sufficiently wide in its meaning to cover the matters in question, there is no need to add synonyms in the hope that the repetition of the same thing will, in some way, reinforce the meaning. The synonyms are an unnecessary belt and braces job. For example, the power to amend the rules of a company pension scheme is sometimes expressed as a power to 'alter, amend, modify, vary or revoke' provisions in the rules. The words 'alter', 'modify, vary or revoke' do not add anything to 'amend', and ought to be deleted.

(b) Habit. Strings of synonyms are often used out of habit, with little or no thought as to whether they achieve any useful purpose. This usually occurs because the drafter has found them in some old precedent or legal document and has adopted them without question. Their use in earlier documents is insufficient reason to continue to use them.

(c) Other parties insist on them. The words used in a legal document may, in some instances, be the result of long negotiations between two or more parties. In such instances, one party may accept words proposed by another party as part of a trade off, even though those words contain unnecessary strings of synonyms in the knowledge that the synonyms do not add to the effect of the clause accepted.

5.10.3 Synonyms commonly used

There is little difficulty in finding a legal document which is well padded with synonyms. The following lists contain examples of synonyms frequently found in legal documents. In all the examples given, one of the words used would be sufficient.

Two words

act and deed

agreed and declared

alienate and set over

all and every

authorise and direct

authorise and empower

bind and obligate

claim and demand

covenant and agree

deed and assurance

do and perform

due and owing

final and conclusive

fit and proper

from and after

full and complete

furnish and supply

goods and chattels

have and hold

if and when

loans and advances

null and void

over and above

power and authority

release and discharge

repair and make good

rules and regulations

save and except

sell and assign

settle and compromise

sole and exclusive

suffer or permit

terms and conditions

true and correct

Three words

amend, vary or modify

build, erect or construct

business, enterprise or undertaking

changes, variations and modifications

costs, charges and expenses

do, execute and perform

give, devise and bequeath

goods, chattels and effects

initiate, institute and commence

lands, tenements and hereditaments

legal, valid and binding

liberties, rights and privileges

loans, borrowings and advances

place, install or affix

reconstitution, reorganisation or reconstruction

rest, residue and remainder

right, title and interest

sell, call in and convert

suit, claim or demand

terminate, cancel and revoke

terms, stipulations and conditions

5.11   Negatives

5.11.1   Use of negatives in drafting

Many concepts can be expressed in either a positive or a negative form. The negative form is often used as a device of understatement and it involves the use of the double negative. For example:

> He was driving at a not inconsiderable speed.

Or:

> John does not attend very often.

Or:

> Mary is not very well.

These statements are indirect in their meaning and if expressed directly in the positive form would be:

> He was driving fast.
>
> John rarely attends.
>
> Mary is unwell.

5.11.2   Use of the positive

As a general rule, the use of the negative should be avoided in drafting. This is because it will often result in the statement of a concept in an indirect manner, with the result that the meaning will not be conveyed as effectively as it should be. It is also likely that the expression of a concept in the positive sense will involve the use of fewer words.

> For example:

> £10,000 to my children, other than those who have not attained age 18.

This clause is clearer in the positive form:

> £10,000 to such of my children as have attained age 18.

A further example is:

> An employee is eligible to join the Scheme if he or she is not:
>
> (a)   under age 22 or over age 60; and
>
> (b)   a casual or a temporary employee.

This would be more direct in the positive form:

> An employee is eligible to join the Scheme if he or she is:
>
> (a)   age 22 and under age 60; and
>
> (b)   a permanent employee.

5.11.3 Use of negatives in mandatory provisions

Sometimes, a provision may direct that a thing is prohibited or that a condition precedent must be performed before a right is acquired. In these cases, the use of the negative is appropriate. For example:

> The trustees shall not invest trust funds in ABC plc.

> The employee shall not bring any alcoholic beverages to his or her place of work.

> No amendment may be made by the Trustees without the prior written consent of the Employer.

5.12   Active and passive voice

5.12.1 What is voice?

In grammar, voice is concerned with how the action of a sentence is viewed. The verb phrase used may be in either the active voice or the passive voice. For example:

> The robber shot the shopkeeper.

And:

> The shopkeeper was shot by the robber.

In each sentence, the facts reported are the same. However, in the first sentence they are reported in the active voice, whilst in the second they are in the passive voice.

5.12.2 Voice in drafting

The active voice should be used where possible in drafting legal documents. This is because verbs which express the legal action in a legal sentence should make it clear who has the duty to perform the legal action and will do so if they are placed near the reference to the person who has to perform the legal action. For example:

> My executors shall pay the sum of £10,000 to my son, Peter.

If this clause were drafted in the passive it would appear as:

> My son, Peter, shall be paid £10,000 by my executors.

The use of the passive may not cause undue difficulty to the reader in short provisions, but, where a provision is long and subject to qualifications and conditions, the use of the passive may result in the references to the duty to be performed, and the person who is to perform it, being separated by the qualifications and conditions and the clause will lose some of its effect. For example, the rules of a company pension scheme may provide for the payment of a spouse's pension on the death of a member in certain circumstances. The clause should be drafted in the active voice as follows:

> Subject to the conditions in this clause, the Trustees shall pay a pension to the spouse of a Member who dies in service ...

The following form of passive drafting does not have the same effect:

> If a Member dies in service and leaves a spouse the spouse shall receive a pension subject to the conditions set out in this clause and which shall be paid by the Trustees.

5.13   Gender

5.13.1 General matters

In English nouns, gender indicates sex or the absence of sex. There are four genders, namely:

(a) Masculine gender, which refers to male human beings, for example, son, husband.

(b) Female gender, which refers to female human beings, for example, daughter, wife.

Masculine and female gender may also refer to male or female animals, for example, bull, cow, cock hen.

(c) Neuter gender, which refers to objects without sex, for example, car, house, light, table.

(d) Common gender, which refers to human beings or animals of either sex, for example, child, adult, bird, sheep, pig.

The masculine and feminine gender may be indicated in three ways. First, through the use of different words for each, for example, brother and sister, father and mother, or goose and gander. Secondly, gender may be indicated by a changed termination, for example, waiter and waitress, testator and testatrix or widow and widower. Third;y, gender may be indicated by the addition of a word to another which is either neuter gender or common gender, for example, policeman and policewoman, landlord and landlady or billy goat and nanny goat.

5.13.2 Gender-neutral language

There is an increasing trend in the use of English to avoid sex bias, although, as Gower points out in *The Complete Plain Words*, 'present usage on such matters is unstable'. Gender-neutral nouns and pronouns are being increasingly used so that terms in the masculine gender are now also applied to women. For example, the term 'chairman' is changed to 'chairperson' or 'chair', depending on taste. Other techniques which are used to make language gender-neutral include:

- replacing 'he' and 'she' with 'he/she' or even 's/he', 'him' and 'her' with 'him/her' and 'man' and 'woman' with 'wo/man';

- the use of gender-neutral pronouns to replace pronouns in the masculine or feminine gender such as 'he' and 'she' and 'him', 'his' and 'hers', so that references are to 'I' and 'we', 'mine' and 'ours', 'me' and 'us' and 'they', 'theirs' and 'them';

- replacing words which terminate with 'man' with some other term which is considered gender-neutral, so that 'postman' becomes 'postal worker', 'fireman' becomes 'firefighter' and 'foreman' becomes 'supervisor';

- using nouns in the common gender in place of nouns in the masculine or feminine gender so that, for example, 'partner' is used to replace 'husband' and 'wife', with the added advantage of covering cases where marital status is unknown; and 'landowner' or 'lessor' is used in place of 'landlord' and 'landlady';

- avoiding expressions which contain a sex bias, for example, 'members of the weaker sex'.

5.13.3 Masculine gender traditional in drafting

The traditional approach to gender in legal drafting is to draft in the masculine gender, regardless of whether a document concerns the rights and obligations of only men or both men and women.

Leaving aside other systemic historical and social factors, the use of the masculine gender in drafting is probably primarily influenced by two factors. First, in legislative drafting, the masculine gender is used. Section 6(a) of the Interpretation Act 1978 provides that, in statutes, 'words importing the masculine gender shall include the feminine'. This approach is frequently mirrored in legal documents by the insertion of an interpretation clause, which may state:

... words denoting one gender shall include all genders ...

Or:

> ... unless the context otherwise determines, words (other than the
> word 'male') importing the masculine gender shall include the
> feminine gender ...

Secondly, the use of the masculine gender was more appropriate in
earlier times because the vast majority of legal documents were
concerned with rights and obligations between men. However, the
continued use of the masculine gender is difficult to justify where,
as is frequently the case, a legal document affects the rights and
obligations of both men and women. For example, with joint
ownership of the matrimonial home by husbands and wives,
contracts for the sale of such property ought to use gender-neutral
language wherever possible. Similarly, the rules of a company
pension scheme should use gender-neutral language as far as
possible when it affects the rights and obligations of both male and
female members. In transactions between women, the use of the
feminine gender or gender-neutral language should be used.
Indeed, in some instances, the use of the masculine gender would
be clearly inappropriate and, in the following example from a
company pension scheme, the feminine gender must be used:

> If a Member is temporarily absent because of pregnancy or
> childbirth then, unless she has given notice of her intention to
> return to work under the Employment Protection (Consolidation)
> Act 1978, Rule 15 shall apply to her.

5.13.4 Use of gender-neutral language in drafting

The lawyer risks criticism in using the masculine gender in drafting
a legal document which affects the rights of both men and women,
since many women may resent being referred to as men. Although
the lawyer should seek to use gender-neutral language where
possible, circumstances may arise where it is not possible or
appropriate to do so, including:

- where the client makes it clear that the masculine gender is to
  be used;

- where a precedent is used as the foundation of a document and is drafted in the masculine gender. In the absence of clear instructions of the client, the constraints of time, or costs, or both, may rule out the possibility of the lawyer going through the document to ensure that it is expressed in gender-neutral language throughout;

- in amending existing documents which are in the masculine gender, the amendments should be in the masculine gender (unless the client gives instructions to change it to gender-neutral language), otherwise the document will become a confusing mixture of different styles.

As a general rule, the client should be invited to set out his or her preferences, but gender-neutral language can be presented/suggested as the 'norm'.

5.13.5 Drafting using gender-neutral pronouns

Drafting in gender-neutral language can be difficult. If, as is often the case, the drafter is inclined to draft in the masculine gender, a conscious effort must be made to avoid lapsing into the masculine gender, especially if the document is long. A further problem is that a clause drafted in gender-neutral language can appear awkward if it follows the syntax which would be used if the clause were drafted in the masculine gender. In many cases, drafting in gender-neutral language may require adaptation of some clauses drafted in the masculine gender. Experience is likely to show that the simplest method of drafting in gender-neutral language is with the use of gender-neutral pronouns throughout a document, so that references are made to 'you' and 'we' and 'us'. This style may not be acceptable in all forms of legal drafting or to all clients. However, a finance company would generally regard it as appropriate to set out the terms of a standard form of agreement for the hire of goods to a consumer. The following example sets out the provisions relating to breach of contract that might be found in a consumer agreement in the masculine gender and using gender-neutral pronouns.

Version 1: masculine gender

6   Breach of contract

    6.1   If the Consumer is in breach of any of the terms or conditions of the contract the Company may give him written notice to terminate the same and recover the Equipment from him.

    6.2   The Company may terminate the contract if the Consumer is at any time the subject of a bankruptcy order, or if he has become insolvent or made any arrangement or composition or assignment for the benefit of his creditors or if any of his assets are subject to any form of seizure.

    6.3   The contract is regulated by the Consumer Credit Act 1974 and a notice to terminate the contract may be served by the Company on the Consumer if he does not comply with the relevant default notice by the date specified in the same which will not be less than seven days.

    6.4   The Company reserves the right to terminate the contract at any time:

Version 2: gender-neutral language

6   Breach of contract

    6.1   If you do not comply with the requirements of this contract we can terminate it and recover the Equipment by giving you written notice.

    6.2   We can also terminate this contract if you are the subject of a bankruptcy order, or if you have become insolvent or make any arrangement or composition or assignment for the benefit of your creditors or if any of your assets are subject to any form of seizure.

    6.3   This contract is regulated by the Consumer Credit Act 1974 and our notice to terminate it takes effect if you do not comply with the relevant default notice by the date specified in it, which may not be less than seven days.

    6.4   Even if we ignore one breach by you of this contract, we can still terminate it if you are in breach of contract again later.

5.13.6 Other examples of drafting in gender-neutral language

As indicated, the use of gender-neutral pronouns to refer to the parties in a legal document is not the traditional approach. For example, the administrative provisions of settlement are usually expressed in the masculine gender, but as is indicated in the example below there is no reason why they should not be expressed in gender-neutral language. The clause deals with trustees' remuneration.

Version 1: masculine gender

> Any trustee being a person engaged in any profession or business shall be entitled to be paid and retain all usual professional or proper charges and commissions for business done by him or by his firm in connection with the trusts of this settlement including any acts which a trustee not being in any profession or business could have done personally.

Version 2: gender-neutral language

> If you are engaged in any profession or business you shall be entitled to be paid and retain all your usual professional or proper charges and commission for any business done by you or your firm or business in connection with this settlement and including any acts which you could have done personally if you had not been in any profession or business.

Gender-neutral language can be found to fit with the formal style of drafting appropriate to many documents. The following provision is from the rules of a members' club and concerns arrears of annual subscription:

> If any member shall fail to pay his annual subscription within one month after it has become due, notice shall be sent to him by post drawing his attention to his failure to pay, and, if he shall not pay the amount within 14 days of the posting of such notice, he may immediately be posted in the club premises as a defaulter. If his annual subscription is not paid one month of the posting of such notice, the committee may terminate his membership.

The clause could be drafted using the plural rather than the singular and, in this way, avoid the use of masculine pronouns. However, the use of the plural means that the clause becomes general in its language, because there is a switch from the active voice to the passive voice. Consequently, it does not make specific reference to the member. This style of drafting requires care, as it may result in a failure to spell out clearly on whom rights, powers or privileges are conferred or on whom obligations or liabilities are imposed:

> Members who fail to pay their annual subscription within one month after it has become due shall be sent a notice by post drawing attention to their failure to pay, and, if the amount is not paid within 14 days of the posting of such notice, they may immediately be posted in the club premises as a defaulter. If the annual subscription is not paid one month of the posting of such notice, the committee may terminate membership.

Another method is to use nouns throughout, so that, in this example, reference is made to the 'member'. This can bring precision which is lacking in using the plural but results in repetition:

> If the annual subscription due from a member is not paid by the member within one month after it has become due, notice shall be sent by post to the member drawing attention to the member's failure to pay, and, if the amount due is not paid within 14 days of the posting of such notice, the member may immediately be posted in the club premises as a defaulter. If the member's annual subscription is not paid one month of the posting of such notice, the committee may terminate the member's membership.

5.13.7   Other possible problems with gender-neutral language

In some circumstances, attempts to use gender-neutral language may give rise to problems because it may add to the length of the document, or result in a style which may not be acceptable to the client. For example, the administrative provisions in a will are likely to refer to 'the executors', whilst the feminine equivalent would be 'the executrix'. If the testator (or testatrix) has appointed a man and a woman to administer his (or her) estate, the alternatives are:

- to be gender-neutral and use the term 'the Personal Representatives'; or
- to refer everywhere to 'the Executor/Executrix'; or
- to use gender-neutral pronouns such as 'you' throughout the document.

The first alternative would include 'administrators/administratrix' and may be too wide for the purposes of some provisions. The second alternative adds to the length of the document and gives it a cumbersome appearance, and begs the question whether the terms should be expressed as 'Executrix/Executor'. The third alternative is unlikely to be acceptable to many clients in a solemn document such as a will, although they may be appropriate in setting out the terms of a sale agreement. These difficulties and the problems of omission which could result from using gender-neutral language may lead the drafter to draft in the masculine and insert an interpretation clause so that the masculine includes the feminine.

5.14   Date and time

5.14.1 Importance

References to date and time are very important in legal documents. Apart from the need to date a document when it is executed in order to indicate the date from which it is effective (although note that a different date may be referred to in the document for some or all of its provisions becoming effective), date and time may play a crucial part in indicating when rights, powers or privileges and obligations or duties commence or end and their duration. Some examples where date and time are important include:

- leases – to indicate the date when the lease commences or expires or its duration;
- contracts of employment – to indicate the contractual period of employment, its commencement and expiry or the period of notice to be given to terminate the contract;

- contracts for the sale of land – to indicate the date of completion;

- trusts – to indicate the date, time or age at which a beneficiary will be entitled to property;

- insurance proposals and policies – to indicate cancellation periods and the period of cover and its commencement and expiry;

- contracts – to indicate when a party must perform under the contract;

- pension plans – to indicate the date on which pensions or other benefits will be payable.

Normally, references to date and time should be expressed with precision, so that there can be no doubt when rights, powers or privileges and obligations or duties begin and end. For example, the date when a lease commences and expires should not be open to doubt. However, exceptions do arise where references to date and time are deliberately left vague (see above, 5.3). For example, parties may not have been able to agree on the date or time for the completion of a contract for the sale of a house and reached a compromise that completion should be within a 'reasonable time' after signature of the contract. Similarly, a contract for services may provide that either party may terminate it upon giving 'reasonable notice' to the other party, because a party with a strong bargaining position has insisted on this. Subject to these exceptions, where circumstances dictate that something less than precision is called for, dates and times must be precise.

5.14.2 General rules

Year

The general rule is that a year is a period of 12 calendar months calculated either from 1 January or some other named day and comprising 365 days in an ordinary year and 366 days in a leap year (see *IRC v Hobhouse* [1956] 1 WLR 1393). Thus, in drafting a reference to a period of years, the day on which the period commences or ends, or both, should be stated. For example:

One year beginning on 1 July 2001.

Or:

One year ending on 30 June 2002.

Or:

One year beginning on 1 July 2001 and ending on 30 June 2002.

In company pension schemes, reference to 'years' will be especially important if pension benefits are computed on the basis of salary at retirement and years of service. In this instance, the documents will need to define 'years' of service in detail.

Month

Section 61 of the Law of Property Act 1925 lays down a statutory presumption that, in all deeds, contracts, wills and other instruments coming into force after 1 January 1926, 'month' means calendar month unless the context otherwise requires. Pre-1925 case law states that 'calendar month' means a complete month in the calendar. It also states that a calendar month can be computed from any day in a month to end on the day having the same number in the next month (see *Migoti v Colville* (1879) 4 CPD 233). Where it is necessary to refer to a period of months, for example, 'six months' notice' in a lease or 'three months' notice' in a contract of employment, it is advisable to indicate the date on which the notice commences and ends in order to avoid any ambiguity. Thus, for example, a lease may refer to:

Six months' notice commencing on 1 July and ending on 31 December.

Alternatively, the period of notice might be given in days rather than months.

Day

A day is the minimum period of time in law and no account is taken of a fraction of a day. The operation of this rule is well illustrated by *Cartwright v MacCormack* [1963] 1 WLR 18, in which an insurance company issued a temporary cover note for motor insurance for 'fifteen days from the commencement of the date of risk'. The note was issued at 11.45 am on 2 December 1959. The insured had an accident at 5.45 pm on 17 December 1959. The insurer argued the policy ran from 11.45 am on 2 December 1959 to 11.45 am on 17 December 1959. This was rejected, since 11.45 only referred to the time the insurance became effective and the 15 days began at midnight on 2 December and, therefore, ended at midnight on 17 December.

5.14.3 Use of expressions 'before' and 'after'

As the examples above illustrate, sometimes times and dates are expressed in legal documents in a way which may lead to difficulties. As a general rule, the use of 'after' and 'before' to express dates will avoid ambiguity. For example:

Employees born after 1 January 1980.

Employees born before 1 January 1980.

Sometimes, dates and times are expressed carelessly and do not meet the intentions behind a provision. For example:

Employees born on 1 January 1980.

Strictly construed, this clause would only apply to employees born on 1 January 1980 – which would be unduly narrow – or employees who were born on or before that date. The words do not express the intention clearly if the intention was to refer to employees born on or before that date.

If 'after' and 'before' are used in the same document, care should be taken to ensure that they do not result in an accidental omission or in overlap. For example, definitions may state:

'Class A Members' means members admitted before 31 December 2000.

'Class B Members' means members admitted after 1 January 2001.

These definitions do not include members who were admitted on or after 31 December 2000 and on or before 1 January 2001. Clearly, there has been an omission. Overlap can also arise in the use of 'after' and 'before'. For example:

On or after 1 December 2000.

On or before 1 December 2000.

This can occur where, for example, the rights of employees are set out in different parts of the same document by reference to when they became employees. If 'on' is used in each clause, persons who became employees on 1 December 2000 will fall into both classes.

5.14.4 Other expressions used in stipulating date and time

The following expressions should be used with care in expressing date and time:

- 'by'

    A notice to quit 'by 1 January' will give the tenant the right to remain in the property until midnight on 1 January. This statement of the date would be incorrect if the landlord had intended that the tenant should be out on 31 December.

- 'from'

    Where a notice is given 'from' a specified date, that day will not be included in the computation. For example, a rent increase effective 'from 25 March' will only take effect on 26 March.

- 'on'

    If a period of time is expressed to begin on a stated day, that day is included. For example, a tenancy which is to commence 'on 15 July' will begin on that day.

● 'till' and 'until'

The cases show that both 'till' and 'until' may be construed by the courts as either inclusive or exclusive. Consequently, they should not be used to express times and dates. For example, if an insurance policy is stated to be effective 'until 1 September', 'until' may mean that it expires at midnight on 31 August or that 1 September is included so that it expires at midnight on 1 September.

● 'between'

If time is expressed as 'between' two dates, the dates mentioned will not be included. For example, 'between 1 January 2000 and 30 June 2003 does not include 1 January 2000 or 30 June 2003. 'Between' is sometimes used to refer to age, and in this respect it may lead to unexpected results. For example, a clause in a trust referring to the settlor's children 'between the ages of 18 and 21 years' would not include children aged exactly 18 or exactly 21 and may, in fact, only include children aged 19 and 20. The uncertainty could be resolved by drafting the provision as 'aged not less than 18 years or more than 21 years'.

5.15   State expressly who has a right, power or duty

When a right, power or duty is set out in a legal document, it should indicate clearly who has the right, power or duty, rather than leave the reader to guess who may have it. In some cases where the holder of the right, power or duty is not named or alluded to, it may be obvious who possesses it, but in other cases this may be virtually impossible to determine. Thus, for example, if the power of investment in a trust deed begins:

The property subject to these trusts may be invested in ...

and then goes on to state the type of investments which may be made without indicating who has the power, it may reasonably be inferred that the power is vested in the trustees of the trust. However, if the trust deed of a company pension scheme states:

A trustee may resign by giving written notice of his resignation ...

it is not clear to whom the notice should be given. In the context of the scheme, it may be arguable that it should be given to the employer in relation to the scheme, or to the trustees of the scheme, or to both.

CHAPTER

6 The Composition of Clauses

Proper words in proper places, make the true definition of a style.

Jonathan Swift (1720)

6.1 Objectives in composing clauses

6.1.1 General points

Drafting is not just a matter of choosing appropriate words to convey the concepts to be embodied in each clause in a legal document, or presenting the concepts in a way that is inviting to the reader. These considerations, although important, will not necessarily result in clear and accurate statements. The manner in which the words in each clause are arranged is equally important.

As in ordinary writing, attention must be given to the arrangement of words (that is, syntax) to ensure that they do not, because of their arrangement, lead to ambiguity or inaccuracy. The principles applicable to syntax in ordinary writing are equally applicable in legal drafting. (See Fowler's *The King's English*, Chapter 2.) Factors which are particularly important in legal drafting include:

- identifying the necessary components of provisions which confer rights, powers or privileges or obligations or liabilities and ensuring they are presented in the most effective manner;

- expressing the document in the correct tense;

- the proper use of punctuation;

- an awareness of the rules of construction which could alter the meaning of the words employed in a clause.

6.1.2 One clause, one concept

Each clause in a legal document should contain only one concept. A clause which combines two or more concepts is likely to make difficult reading, especially if each concept is long and subject to some exceptions or conditions. There is a danger that, where two or more concepts are included in one clause, important qualifications or conditions may be omitted or imprecisely expressed. If the concepts have no obvious relationship, the reader may wrongly conclude otherwise and misunderstand. For example, a clause in a trust deed dealing with the appointment and removal of trustees, and also with the trustees' powers to delegate, is liable to be confusing. A separate clause should be used for appointment and removal and for delegation. Even if a clause is paragraphed, the inclusion of two concepts within it is inappropriate, as important provisions may be overlooked by the reader. One test which can be applied to ensure that only one concept is included is to check that the contents fall within the heading or short title to the clause.

6.2 Components of clauses

6.2.1 Coode's elements

One of the earliest writers on legal composition was George Coode. His paper, 'On legislative expression, or the language of the written law' was first printed as an introduction to the Appendix annexed to the Report of the Poor Law Commissioners on Local Taxation in 1843. Although his analysis dealt with legislative composition, it is also of considerable value in drafting legal documents, because the objectives are similar in each case. In relation to legislative composition, Coode observed:

> There is an acknowledged, indeed an obvious, distinction between the three operations of determining the final objects or policy of a law, of choosing the means for the attainment of those objects, and of enunciating that choice by means of language. Though the last process is subordinate, and is only executory of the two former, it does, like all executory functions, according as they are well or ill

performed, fix the limits within which the superior function will operate.

Legal documents are law for the parties whom they affect and, therefore, should follow similar principles. For example, the rules of a club regulate the rights and obligations of the members and those who manage the club, whilst a lease regulates the rights and obligations of the landlord and the tenant. Since, in each case, the provisions in the legal document regulate the rights and obligations of the parties, they must be composed in a way which will ensure accuracy and clarity.

6.2.2   Coode's analysis

Coode explained the elements of legislative expression in the following terms:

THE EXPRESSION of every law essentially consists of,

– 1st, the description of *the legal Subject*;

– 2dly, the enunciation of *the legal Action*.

To these, when the law is not of universal application, are to be added,

– 3dly, the description of *the Case* to which the legal action is confined; and,

– 4thly, *the Conditions* on performance of which the legal action operates.

Coode viewed the law as imposing rights, privileges or powers and corresponding liabilities and obligations on those who must confer the rights, privileges or powers. The four elements in detail are:

(a) The legal subject

The legal subject is the person on whom a right, privilege or power is conferred or a liability or obligation is imposed. Coode said:

Now, no Right, Privilege or Power can be conferred, and no Obligation or Liability imposed, otherwise than on some person.

The PERSON who may or may not or shall or shall not do something or submit to something is the legal subject of the legal action.

This principle remains valid today. It is vital that a legal sentence should identify the person who is to take the legal action. For example:

The buyer shall pay to the seller the purchase price on 1 December 2001.

The legal subject, namely the buyer, is identified in relation to the duty he must perform (the legal action), that is, payment of the purchase price. The sentence should not leave the identification of the legal subject to be drawn by inference from other provisions in the document, as in the following example, which does not refer to the vendor:

The purchaser shall receive the purchase price on 1 December 2001.

Some further examples in which the legal subject is referred to in relation to the legal action are:

The Landlord agrees with the Tenant to keep the main structure and electrical and gas supplies in repair and to keep heating and water supply apparatus supplied by the Landlord in repair.

The Trustees may insure against any loss or damage from any peril any property for the time being comprised in the Trust Fund for any amount and pay the premiums out of the Trust Fund.

Contrast these examples with the following clauses which do not identify the legal subject and, therefore, leave uncertainty as to who is to exercise the power or duty:

Notice shall be given in writing.

This clause does not identify the legal subject, that is, the person who must give the notice. It may be possible to infer, from other provisions in the same document, who is supposed to give the notice, but this is undesirable because, in some cases, it could lead to a construction of the clause which is different from that intended. Another example is:

> Trustees may be appointed or removed by deed.

This clause fails to state who is to exercise the power to appoint or remove trustees. It may be obvious to a trusts lawyer that, under s 36 of the Trustee Act 1925, the power is with the trustees, in the absence of any express reference to the person who is to exercise the power. However, this type of drafting is unacceptable because it results in a document which is uninformative to a reader who is unaware of the provisions of the Trustee Act 1925. He will probably need to seek legal advice on who has the power. In many instances, drafting of this kind is the result of carelessness. If, in the last example, the settlor had intended to retain the power of appointment and removal to himself, the act of carelessness would have lost him an important control over the trustees of the settlement. Even if it is unlikely that a failure to refer to the legal subject would result in prejudice to anyone, the habit of referring to the legal subject should be adopted if only to make the contents of the clause clearer and less impersonal and, perhaps, avoid an omission of the legal subject when it is critical. For example:

> Employees will be entitled to maternity/paternity leave.

This would be much clearer if drafted as:

> The Employer shall give Employees maternity/paternity leave.

(b) The legal action

The legal action is a statement of the right, privilege or power or the obligation or liability conferred or imposed on the legal subject. On this, Coode said:

> The *legal action* is that part of every legislative sentence in which the Right, Privilege or Power, or the Obligation or Liability, is defined, wherein it is said that a person *may* or *may not*, or *shall* or *shall not* do any act, or shall submit to some act.

> As the *legal subject* defines the *extent* of the law, so the description of the *legal action* expresses the nature of the law. It expresses all that the law effects as law.

Coode was of the opinion that the legal subject and the legal action were the essential elements of every legal sentence and without them, no law could be written. Again, this point remains valid today. For example:

> The Employer will engage the Employee as a sales manager.

In this sentence, the only elements are the legal subject and the legal action. These are:

- legal subject: the Employer;
- legal action: will engage the Employee as a sales manager.

Another example in which the only elements are the legal subject and the legal action is:

> My Executors shall pay £10,000 to X.

- Legal subject: my Executors;
- legal action: shall pay £10,000 to X.

A failure to state the legal action fully is not uncommon. For example:

> The seller may terminate the contract by giving notice.

It is likely that the notice must be given to the buyer, but the clause should have stated this. The clause should also have stated the period of notice to be given and whether it should be written.

Coode also pointed out that the legal action should be clearly apparent on a preliminary consideration of the sentence. He said:

> The *legal action* should immediately appear on inspection of the sentence. No good enactment requires to be covered up in deceptive language, or involved in a preamble, or got by implication from terms used in the description of the legal subject ...

(c) The case

The case is a statement of the circumstances in which a provision is to operate. Coode advised that the case to which the clause is confined should be expressed at the beginning of a sentence, because it would be misleading to begin a provision in a way which indicated that it was of universal application and to conclude with qualifications or provisos which restricted its scope. A reader would only discover at the end of the clause whether it was applicable and, if it was not, would have wasted time in reading it. He said:

> ... wherever the law is intended to operate only in certain circumstances, those circumstances should be invariably described BEFORE any other part of the enactment is expressed.

Coode then added bluntly:

> If this rule were observed nine-tenths of the wretched provisos, and after limitations and qualifications with which the law is disfigured and confused, would be avoided, and no doubt could ever possibly arise, except through the bad choice of terms, as to the occasions in which the law applied, and in which it did not.

As Coode indicates, the case states the circumstances which must arise before a provision can operate. It is only when the legal subject is to perform the legal action in limited circumstances that the case must be stated. For example:

> My Trustees shall pay my son, John, £50,000.

This clause comprises only the legal subject and the legal action which are:

- legal subject: my Trustees;
- legal action: shall pay my son, John, £50,000.

If the payment is to be made in particular circumstances, such as John attaining age 21, this would represent the case. The clause might be drafted as follows:

> When my son, John, attains the age of 21 years my Trustees shall pay him the sum of £50,000.

This clause may be analysed as follows:

- case: when my son, John, attains the age of 21 years;
- legal subject: my Trustees;
- legal action: shall pay him the sum of £50,000.

Despite Coode's advice, sometimes – especially where the clause is a short one – it will be appropriate to place the case at the end of the clause. For example:

> My trustees shall pay the sum of £50,000 to my son, John, when he attains the age of 21.

The following clauses are to operate only in the circumstances set out as the case at the beginning of each clause. The first is from a credit-token agreement, and relates to loss or misuse of a credit card, while the second is from a contract of employment and deals with absence through sickness:

> If a card is lost or stolen or a card is for any other reason liable to be misused, you must immediately notify us.

This clause may be analysed as:

- case: if a card is lost or stolen or a card is for any other reason liable to be misused;
- legal subject: you;
- legal object: must immediately notify us.

> In the event of absence on account of sickness or injury the Employee (or someone on his behalf) must inform the Employer of the reason for the Employee's absence not later than the end of the working day on which absence first occurs.

This may be analysed as:

- case: in the event of absence on account of sickness or injury;
- legal subject: the Employee (or someone on his behalf);
- legal action: must inform the Employer of the reason for the Employee's absence not later than the end of the working day on which absence first occurs.

(d) The conditions

This is a statement of any conditions or restrictions which must be satisfied before a provision applies. Coode said of conditions:

> A *law* ... may ... operate only on the performance by some person of certain conditions. It is not till something has been done that the right can be enjoyed, or that compliance with the obligation can be enforced, or that the liability can be applied.

The following clauses contain conditions which must be satisfied before the legal subject must or may perform the legal action. In addition, each clause contains the case and, therefore, comprises all four elements of legislative expression:

> Where the Tenant fails to execute a repair specified in a notice served under clause 12 hereof, the Landlord or his agents may enter the premises and carry out that repair.

- Case: where the Tenant fails to execute a repair;
- condition: specified in a notice served under clause 12 hereof;
- legal subject: the Landlord or his agents;
- legal action: may enter the premises and carry out that repair.

A further example is:

> Where the seller terminates the contract because he is unable to supply the goods, the seller will refund to the buyer all sums paid by the buyer under the contract.

- Case: where the seller terminates the contract;
- condition: because he is unable to supply the goods;
- legal subject: the seller;
- legal action: will refund to the buyer all sums paid by the buyer under the contract.

Coode pointed out that conditions should be drafted with care so that they do not import either more or less by way of condition than is necessary. Too much by way of condition could defeat the acquisition of rights or imposition of obligations, whilst too little could result in rights being obtained too readily or obligations being imposed in onerous circumstances. In either instance, the client's instructions would not have been followed.

6.2.3   Use of Coode's elements

Coode's elements of legislative expression are a useful basis for constructing legal provisions which are intended to confer rights, powers or privileges, or to impose obligations or liabilities. However, it should also be borne in mind that modern legal documents also contain provisions which are not intended to confer rights, powers or privileges or impose obligations or liabilities, but are declaratory of matters which relate to them. Clauses which set out definitions are an example in point, as are the following clauses:

(a) Clause on proper law and jurisdiction

> This agreement shall be governed by English law in every way including formation and interpretation.

(b) Perpetuity clause from Wills Trusts

> The perpetuity period applicable to these trusts shall be 80 years commencing on the date of my death.

(c) Service of notices under a lease

> The provisions of the Law of Property Act 1925 as amended by the Recorded Delivery Service Act 1962 applies to the giving and service of all notices and documents in relation to this lease.

Sometimes, a clause may set out a list of legal actions which are to be performed by a party. In order to reduce the length of the document, the legal subject may only be referred to at the beginning of the clause and each legal action set out in a sub-clause with any relevant case or conditions. Although this approach is not entirely in line with Coode's analysis, it is an attractive means of conveying information to a reader, especially if the clause is paragraphed. For example:

The Landlord agrees:

(1) to give the Tenant possession of the Property at the Commencing Date of the Tenancy;

(2) to maintain the Property in good order and repair;

(3) not to interfere with the Tenant's right peacefully to occupy the Property except for access to inspect the condition of the Property or to carry out repairs to the Property or adjoining property;

(4) on payment of the sum of £180 per month by the Tenant, to provide a gardener to maintain the gardens at the Property.

6.3   Tense

6.3.1   Introduction

There should be consistency in the use of tense in the drafting of legal documents, as in any writing. A legal provision which jumps from past to present to future tense will make difficult reading and may even be ambiguous. Statutes are drafted in the present indicative tense. As Lopes LJ said in *Re Pulborough Parish School Board Election* [1894] 1 QB 725, p 737:

> It is a well recognised principle in the construction of statutes that they operate only on cases and facts which come into existence after the statutes were passed, unless a retrospective effect was clearly intended.

A perusal of any statute will reveal the use of present tense. For example, s 2(2) of the Occupiers' Liability Act 1957 states:

> The common duty of care is a duty to take such care as in all the circumstances of the case is reasonable to see that the visitor will be reasonably safe in using the premises for the purposes for which he is invited or permitted by the occupier to be there.

Section 2(1) of the Animals Act 1971 states:

> Where any damage is caused by an animal which belongs to a dangerous species, any person who is a keeper of the animal is liable for the damage, except as is otherwise provided by this Act.

6.3.2   Use of present tense in legal documents

The present tense should be used in drafting legal documents. The reasons behind the use of the present tense in statutes were explained by Coode, and are equally applicable in drafting legal documents. He said:

> If the law be regarded while it remains in force as *constantly speaking*, we get a clear and simple rule of expression, which will, whenever a case occurs for its application, accurately correspond with the then state of facts. The law will express in the present tense facts and conditions required to be concurrent with the operation of *the legal action*; in the perfect past tense, facts and conditions required as precedents to *the legal action* ...

He then went on to explain the advantages:

> This mode of expression, assuming the law to be always speaking – reciting facts concurrent with its operation, as if they were present facts, and facts precedent to its operation, as if they were past facts – has two very considerable advantages:
>
> – First, it avoids the necessity of very complicated grammatical construction in the statement of cases and conditions, often involving the use of futures, perfect futures, and past conditionals –
>
>> if a person *shall* be convicted of, &c; and if he *shall have been* before convicted of the same offence; and if he *shall* not *have* undergone the punishment which he *should have undergone* for the offence of which he *shall have been so before convicted*.
>
> – Secondly, keeping the description of *cases* and *conditions* in the present and in the perfect tenses, it leaves the imperative and potential language of *the legal action* clearly distinguished, by the broadest and most intelligible forms of expression. Narration will appear in narrative language, instead of being allowed, as now, to usurp imperious language, and thus to confound *the facts* and *the law*.

6.3.3 Drafting in the present tense

Coode's advice on drafting in the present tense is frequently overlooked in the drafting of legal documents. One reason for this is because 'shall' is used to excess. As is indicated below, 7.2, 'shall' should be used only in the imperative sense in legal drafting to impose an obligation or duty. The use of 'shall' to imply futurity is not necessary, but is common where a provision contains the case or the condition, as in the following examples:

If the buyer shall give 14 days notice in writing to the seller he may return the goods ...

If the trustee shall in their absolute discretion determine ...

If any balance shall have been found to be due ...

All payments shall be made in such manner as the trustees shall direct ...

If any person shall neglect to ...

These clauses could be redrafted in the present tense using fewer words and without altering their effect as follows:

If the buyer gives 14 days notice in writing to the seller he may return the goods ...

If the trustee in their absolute discretion determine ...

If any balance is found to be due ...

All payments are made in such manner as the trustees direct ...

If any person neglects to ...

6.4   Punctuation

6.4.1   Punctuation is generally not used

In old legal documents, punctuation was rarely used and it was not unusual to find a document which went on for several pages or, indeed, from start to finish, without any full stops, commas or other punctuation. One reason for the lack of punctuation was the concern that a punctuation mark might be construed by the court as altering the meaning of the words used. This was because the case law contained confused signals as to the significance of punctuation in legal documents. In *Houston v Burns* [1918] AC 337, Lord Shaw said:

> Punctuation is a rational part of English composition, and is sometimes quite significantly employed. I see no reason for depriving legal documents of such significance as attaches to punctuation in other writings.

However, in *Gordon v Gordon* (1871) LR 5 HL 254, Lord Westbury treated punctuation in a will he was construing as unimportant, and said:

> My Lords, so far as punctuation is concerned, I believe there is no trace of any punctuation in the original will; but whether that be so or not, I entirely concur in the opinion expressed by Sir William Grant, in a case before him [*Sandford v Raikes*], that 'it is from the words, and not from the context, and not from the punctuation' that the meaning of the testator is to be collected.

Given the ambiguous pronouncements of the courts on punctuation, it is not surprising that many legal documents are still produced with a minimum of punctuation, or even resort to the use of capitals where punctuation might otherwise have been employed. The problems punctuation can cause are illustrated by *Gauntlett v Carter* (1853) 17 Beav 586, in which a testator made a devise of his property 'in Bullen Court, Strand, and in Maiden Lane in the county of Middlesex'. The testator had property in both Bullen Court, which was off the Strand, and in the Strand, and the issue was whether only the property in Bullen Court passed under the devise or this property and the property in the Strand. It was held that both properties passed under the devise. However, the difficulty might have been avoided if express words had been used and punctuation omitted, for example: 'my properties in Bullen Court, Strand and in the Strand and in Maiden Lane ...'

6.4.2   Using punctuation

The omission of all punctuation in drafting hardly fits with ordinary usage and there is a case for its use, even if limited, especially where the contents of the clauses in a document are paragraphed. If it is felt that punctuation may alter the intended meaning of words used, this may be a strong signal that those words ought to be reconsidered, because they should be able to convey their meaning in an unambiguous manner, unassisted by punctuation. As Fowler's *The King's English* advises, 'it may almost be said that what reads wrongly if the stops are removed is radically bad; stops are not to alter meaning but to show it up'. If, for some reason, there is concern as to the effect of punctuation, it could be omitted or dealt with by an express provision in the interpretation section of the document stating:

> Punctuation used in this document is to be ignored in determining the construction of its provisions.

Or:

> If any provision in this document is capable of being interpreted in one way with regard to punctuation used and in another without regard to punctuation used, the latter is to be preferred.

If it is desired that punctuation should be taken into account, the following clauses might be included in the interpretation provisions:

> Punctuation marks are to be given full effect in the construction of this document.

Or:

> If any provision in this document is capable of being interpreted in one way with regard to punctuation used and in another without regard to punctuation used, the former is to be preferred.

6.4.3   What punctuation should be used?

If punctuation is used in a legal document, it should be kept to a minimum. Too much punctuation is likely to mar the presentation of the document. As in ordinary English usage, there are different views on how punctuation ought to be used in legal documents. The following rules might be adopted. They are based on the use of punctuation in statutes:

- full stops should be used at the end of sections and sub-sections;

- items of enumeration are separated by semi-colons unless the enumeration is to facilitate reading, in which case a comma is used at the end of each item;

- a comma or dash is used to separate the introductory words from the items of an enumeration;

- a comma is used to separate the last item of an enumeration from any words which follow;

- quotation marks are used around terms defined in the definitions section;

- parentheses are used where necessary information is introduced into a clause;

- question marks and exclamation marks are not used;

- where a clause begins with the case, condition or both, these are separated from the main part of the clause by a comma.

6.5   Words and spelling

6.5.1   General

Words and phrases continually fall into disuse and eventually become archaic. Reference has been already been made (above, 5.8) to the use of archaic language. New words and phrases constantly enter the English language. Some are invented to refer to new things, for example, cashpoint, AIDS, bond washing, etc, while others are derived from other languages, for example, Glasnost and jojoba, or from other varieties of English usage in the US, Canada or Australia. It is advisable that a legal document drafted with the object that it should be subject to English law be composed in what Gower's *The Complete Plain Words* calls 'British English', and should avoid words or terms which are not in general use in British English. In addition, words and terms which are used only in a particular dialect in the UK should be avoided.

6.5.2   Avoid foreign words and phrases

Gower's *The Complete Plain Words* advises:

> The safest rule about foreign words and phrases ... is to avoid them if you can. This is partly because you may easily use them wrongly and partly because ... your reader may be less learned than you and must not be made to feel inferior.

This advice applies as much to legal composition as to ordinary writing. Where words or phrases which are foreign in origin have become part of 'British English', the drafter must decide if they are sufficiently unusual as to be meaningless to, or misunderstood by, the intended reader. For example, words such as garage, hotel and restaurant passed into general English usage long ago, but words such as pied-à-terre and détente might be best avoided.

6.5.3   Other varieties of English

Many words and phrases are used in other varieties of English in place of words and phrases used in British English. American English provides many examples on this point and words and phrases such as buying on time, bill, apartment, ordinance, and legal holiday should not be used in place of their respective British English equivalents of hire purchase, note, flat, bylaw and bank holiday. In some cases, a word or phrase used in another variety of English may have a meaning which is different to that in British English and, if used in a legal document governed by English law, may result in something different from that intended by the parties. For example, a lease of a first floor flat would mean in American English a flat at ground level, whilst in British English it would mean a flat above the ground floor.

6.5.4   Abbreviations of words

Some words are used in everyday speech in an abbreviated form. For example, ad, memo, photo, phone and pub are regularly used in place of advertisement, memorandum, photograph, telephone and public house respectively. The abbreviated form should not be used in drafting unless it has effectively superseded the non-abbreviated form. For example, bus and taxi may be acceptable in place of omnibus and taxicab.

6.5.5   Slang

The advice in Fowler's *The King's English* is 'never to use slang except in dialogue, and there as little as may be'. There is no place for slang in legal documents. A contract of employment would not be of any credit to its author if it referred to 'being sacked' or 'given the boot' instead of 'dismissal', or referred to a salary of '10,000 quid' instead of '£10,000'.

6.5.6   Word formation

Some odd word formations are occasionally encountered in everyday speech or in particular varieties of English. Since they may not be universally understood, they should be avoided in legal drafting. Examples include burglarise, casualise, diarise, hospitalise, traumatisation, legalisation, nominalisations, etc. Sometimes, odd word formations may become acceptable with the passage of time so that their use in legal documents would not lead to misunderstanding, for example, decontaminate or privatisation. However, it is often possible to use alternative words which are shorter or clearer or both so that, for example, 'decontaminate' could be replaced by 'cleanse' and words such as 'non-appearance' and 'defrost' could be replaced by 'absent' and 'thaw' respectively.

6.5.7   Spelling

Spelling in legal documents should follow that used in British English. For example, words such as colour, honour, or surprise should not be spelt as color, honor or surprize, even though this may be acceptable in other varieties of English. Archaic spelling should be avoided, so that negotiate, control and expense should not be spelt in their older forms of negociate, controul and expence. Differences between spelling of words used in their legal rather than general sense should be observed so that, for example, 'judgement' should be spelt as 'judgment' when referring to a decision by a judge. If there is doubt as to the proper spelling of a word, reference should be made to the *Oxford Spelling Dictionary* or to the *Oxford Dictionary*.

6.6 Provisos

6.6.1 Introduction

Many legal documents are cluttered with provisos. They are usually appended to the end of a clause to set out an exception, condition or qualification to the general principle expressed in the clause. To ensure that the proviso cannot be overlooked by the reader, it is often emphasised in capitals and may come in the form PROVIDED THAT; or PROVIDED ALWAYS THAT; or PROVIDED FURTHER THAT; or PROVIDED NEVERTHELESS THAT. The proviso is a relic of the past and should not be used. Even though the proviso is inappropriate today (see below, 6.6.2), its use continues unabated and it appears to have evolved into a multipurpose conjunction in legal documents.

6.6.2 Origin of the proviso

The proviso originated in the drafting of statutes, in which it was used as a term of enactment. Prior to 1850, statutory provisions were not divided into sections and it was necessary for each enactment in a statute to have its own enacting words. Where a qualification or exception was introduced to the general operation of a statute, this was also prefaced by the enacting words, namely, 'it is provided that'. With the passage of time, these words were abbreviated to 'provided that' or variations such as 'provided always'. The need for each enactment, qualification or exception to an enactment to have its own enacting words was abolished by s 11 of the Interpretation of Acts Act 1850, which stated:

> Be it enacted, that all Acts shall be divided into Sections, if there be more Enactments than One, which Sections shall be deemed substantive Enactments, without any introductory words.

The use of provisos in legal documents seems to have originated from their use in statutes and has outlived their use in statutes which ceased after 1850. Legal documents do not need enacting provisions, especially in sub-clauses setting out exceptions or qualifications. It is more appropriate (and clearer) to set out an exception by prefacing it with 'except that' or as a condition with the preface 'on condition that'.

6.6.3   Coode's views

Coode criticised the use of provisos to set out exceptions or qualifications in statutes. His criticisms, although directed towards the use of provisos in statutes, is applicable to their continued use in legal documents. He said:

> IT IS MOST DESIRABLE that the use of the provisos should be kept within some reasonable bounds. It is indeed a question whether there is ever a real necessity for a proviso. At present the abuse of the formula is universal. Formerly they were used in an intelligible manner; – where a general enactment had preceded, but a special case occurred for which a distinct and special enactment was to be made, different from the general enactment, this latter enactment was made by way of proviso ...

> The present use of the proviso by the best draftsmen is very anomalous. It is often used to introduce mere exceptions to the operation of an enactment, where no special provision is made for such exceptions. But it is obvious that such exceptions would be better expressed as exceptions; if particular cases were to be excepted, to be expressed in the case; if particular conditions were dispensed with, to be expressed in the condition: if certain persons were to be excluded from the operation of the enactment, to be

expressed in the subject. In fact, where the enunciation of the general provision is merely to be negatived in some particular, the proper place for the expression of that negation is by an exception expressed in immediate contact with the general words by which the particular would otherwise be included. This would make, in all cases, the definition of the case, condition, subject, or action, complete at once, that is to say, it would show in immediate contact all that is included and all that is excluded ...

Another common use of provisos is to introduce the several stages of consecutive operations. In such cases the words 'provided always' are mere surplusage, or should be replaced by the conjunction 'and' ...

Worse than all the above anomalies, however, is the use commonly made by ordinary draftsmen of the proviso. Wherever matter is seen by the writer to be incapable of being directly expressed in connexion with the rest of any clause, he thrusts it in with a proviso. Whenever he perceives a disparity, an anomaly, an inconsistency, or a contradiction, he introduces it with 'provided always'.

6.6.4   Problems in using provisos

Quite apart from the fact that provisos are anomalous and unnecessary, their use does not assist with clarity in a legal document. If they are used to excess, they may also result in inaccuracy or ambiguity. The following clause is from a lease and it contains an excess of unnecessary provisos:

10   User of premises

The tenant covenants with the landlord not to carry on any trade or business on the demised premises other than the business of a tailor PROVIDED THAT the tenant may apply to the landlord for a change of user and PROVIDED FURTHER THAT the landlord covenants with the tenant that in the event that the tenant applies to the landlord for a change of user the landlord will apply to the head lessor for consent to such change of user and use his best endeavours to obtain the head lessor's consent and forward to the tenant copies of all correspondence he receives from the head lessor in relation to the application for consent to such change of user PROVIDED ALWAYS THAT the tenant pays the costs of the same and PROVIDED FURTHER THAT the landlord covenants with the tenant not to withhold consent to the tenant's application for a change of user if the head lessor consents to the change of user applied for by the landlord under the provisions of this clause.

The provisos have been used in this clause to string together several matters and little thought has been given to their arrangement. They could be omitted and the clause made more readable and accurate if it were paragraphed:

10 User of premises

    (1) The tenant covenants with the landlord not to carry on any trade or business on the demised premises other than the business of a tailor.

    (2) The tenant may apply to the landlord for a change of user.

    (3) In the event that the tenant applies to the landlord for a change of user, the landlord covenants with the tenant, but at the tenant's cost,

        (a) to apply to the head lessor for consent to such change of user;

        (b) to use his best endeavours to obtain the head lessor's consent; and

        (c) to forward to the tenant copies of all correspondence he receives from the head lessor in relation to the application for consent to such change of user.

    (4) If the head lessor consents to a change of user applied for by the landlord in accordance with sub-clause (3), the landlord covenants with the tenant not to withhold consent to the tenant's application for a change of user.

6.6.5 Avoiding provisos

As stated, provisos continue to be used in many modern legal documents even though there is no justification for them. They can only serve to obscure meaning. There are three main cases where they continue to be used, and in each they could be avoided by using alternative (and clearer) words. These are:

(a) Provisos in definitions

Definitions often have provisos tacked onto them which are substantive provisions that ought to appear in the body of the document. This matter has already been referred to above, 4.4.5. The example below, which is taken from the rules of a company pension scheme, illustrates the point:

> 'Overseas Service' means in relation to a Member:
>
> (a)   service in the employment of the Employers outside the UK; or
>
> (b)   secondment by the Employers to service outside the UK either with one of the Employers or otherwise on their behalf,
>
> PROVIDED THAT such service is specified to be for a period not exceeding 36 months or until the trustees have obtained the agreement of the Inland Revenue to the continued participation of the Member in the Scheme.

The material in the proviso is substantive and should have been included in the rule which dealt with the position of an employee in overseas service (which was extensive in the document from which this is taken).

(b) Provisos expressing exceptions or qualifications

An exception or qualification to a general principle is often indicated by 'PROVIDED THAT' or 'PROVIDED ALWAYS THAT'. Exceptions should be preceded by the words 'except that' and conditions by 'on condition that'.

In some instances, the use of paragraphing (referred to above, 3.4) may eliminate the need for provisos, so that the general principle is set out in one clause and the exception or qualification in another clause. The following clause, which is illustrated in three different drafting styles, gives a vendor the right to remove fixtures from a property sold and indicates how provisos can be avoided where exceptions or qualifications arise.

Traditional style with provisos

> The Purchaser agrees with the Vendor to permit the Vendor to remove and take away at his own expense at any time prior to Completion the Adam marble mantelpieces situated in the drawing room and the dining room of the said Property PROVIDED THAT the Vendor at his own expense replaces the same with the mantelpieces to be provided by the Purchaser and makes good all damage occasioned by the removal and replacement of the same which may be caused to the plasterwork decorations other fixtures or otherwise to the fabric of the Property.

Quite apart from the removal of the proviso, the language of the clause could be simplified.

Modern English unparagraphed

> The Buyer agrees with the Seller to permit the Seller to remove at any time prior to Completion the Adam marble mantelpieces in the drawing room and the dining room of the Property on condition that the Seller replaces them with the mantelpieces to be supplied by the Buyer and makes good all damage occasioned by the removal and replacement of the mantelpieces.

Modern English paragraphed

> (1) Subject to paragraph (2) below the Buyer agrees with the Seller to permit the Seller to remove at any time prior to Completion the Adam marble mantelpieces in the drawing room and the dining room of the Property.
>
> (2) The Seller shall,
>
> (a) replace the Adam marble mantelpieces with mantelpieces to be supplied by the Buyer; and
>
> (b) make good all damage caused by the removal and replacement of the mantelpieces.

A further example is a clause taken from a partnership agreement concerning the conduct of the partnership:

> 15 Conduct of partnership
>
> Each partner covenants with the other partners to be bound by decisions of a majority of the partners PROVIDED THAT a decision of the partners affecting a change in the nature of the

> partnership shall be unanimous and PROVIDED FURTHER THAT in the event of an equality of votes on a majority decision of the partners the Senior Partner shall have a casting vote.

This clause includes three separate matters which have been strung together with provisos, that is:

- that decisions of the partners are to be by majority vote;

- that a unanimous vote is required for a change of business; and

- the Senior Partner is to have a casting vote if there is a tie.

The clause does not make easy reading and the contents could be drafted without the provisos, especially if it were paragraphed:

15   Conduct of partnership

   (1)   Subject to sub-clauses (2) and (3) below each partner covenants with the other partners to be bound by decisions of a majority of the partners.

   (2)   A decision of the partners affecting a change in the nature of the partnership business shall be unanimous.

   (3)   If there is an equality of votes on a decision to be made by a majority of the partners the Senior Partner may exercise a casting vote.

(c) Separate clauses

Sometimes, provisos are used to weld together material that should be set in separate clauses. A basic rule is that each clause should deal with only one concept or thought (see above, 6.1.2). If two or more concepts are included in one clause, the clause should be split into two clauses. For example, a will may include a clause which contains both a disposition of property to be held on certain trusts and the administrative provisions relating to the trusts. The administrative provisions should be set out in a separate clause at the end of the will.

The following clause is from a contract for the sale of goods. It deals with acceptance of the goods by the buyer and has a

provision on liability for loss and expense caused by a breach
thrown in at the end:

> The Buyer shall not be deemed to have accepted the Goods or any
> part thereof until the Buyer has inspected the Goods and
> ascertained that they are in accordance with this agreement
> PROVIDED THAT the Buyer may reject the Goods or any part
> thereof which are not in accordance with the agreement within a
> reasonable time after such inspection PROVIDED ALWAYS THAT
> if the Buyer rejects the Goods or any part thereof the Seller agrees
> to accept the return of the Goods or part thereof and refund the
> Price to the Buyer PROVIDED FURTHER THAT the Seller shall be
> under no liability for any loss or expense (including loss of profit)
> suffered by the Buyer arising out of a breach by the Seller of this
> agreement.

The material following the last proviso seems to have been thrust
into this clause, even though it concerns different matters from
those dealt with in the earlier part of the clause. The fact that it may
have been relevant to certain events, for example, if the Seller
should refuse to accept the return of the goods, is insufficient
reason to incorporate it into the clause. It should be in a separate
clause. The clause would also be much improved if it were drafted
without provisos and if it were paragraphed.

6.7   The *ejusdem generis* rule

6.7.1   The rule

Case law is littered with examples which illustrate the difficulties
which can arise when the *ejusdem generis* rule is applied in the
construction of a clause in a legal document. It is for this reason
that the provisions of a document should be drafted so as to avoid
its application. In *Lyndon v Standbridge* (1857) 2 H & N 45, Pollock
CB explained the rule in the following terms:

> It is a general rule of construction that where a particular class is
> spoken of and general words follow, the class first mentioned is to
> be taken as the most comprehensive, and the general words

treated as referring to matters which are *ejusdem generis* with such class.

For example, if a testator made a gift in his will in the following terms:

> I leave all my china, plate, furniture, pictures and other household items at 50 Green Street to my son, Fred,

the words 'other household items' would be construed as *ejusdem generis* with the class of objects described, namely, 'china, plate, furniture, pictures' and items in this class would be included in the gift. Thus, glassware and carpets would be included, as they are in the same class as household items, but business equipment such as computers and documents would not be included. In this example, the general words only avoid the accidental omission of one of the objects of the kind mentioned which could occur if it was sought to draft the gift in exhaustive terms.

6.7.2 Limits of the rule

There are some limits on the application of the *ejusdem generis* rule. The courts have held that it will not be applied in the construction of a document in certain circumstances. However, these exceptions ought not to be relied on in drafting a document, as it may be open to argument whether circumstances for excluding the effect of the rule have arisen. The rule will not apply in the following cases.

(a) No class of objects mentioned

The rule can only apply if the list of items which is followed by general words have a common characteristic which constitutes them a class or genus so that all other things of the same class or genus are swept in by the general words. For example, in *SS Magnhild v Macintyre* [1920] 3 KB 321, the rule was not applied to a provision excluding liability for loss of time from deficiency of men or owner's stores, breakdown of machinery or damage to hull, or other accident preventing the work of the steamer, since these items did not form a class or genus.

(b) Class or genus is exhaustive

The rule will not be applied where the class or genus mentioned is exhaustive. In these circumstances, the general words will be regarded as referring to some larger class or genus.

(c) Commercial documents

The rule may be applied less restrictively in commercial documents. In *Chandris v Isbrandsen-Moller Co Inc* [1951] 1 KB 240, a charterparty provided that cargo was to consist of lawful general merchandise 'excluding acids, explosives, arms, ammunition and other dangerous cargo'. The question arose as to whether a cargo of turpentine was included in the prohibition. Devlin J examined the rule in detail, and concluded that it did not apply to commercial documents:

> The *ejusdem generis* rule means that there is implied into the language which the parties have used words of restriction which are not there. It cannot be right to approach a document with the presumption that there should be such an implication. To apply the rule automatically in that way would be to make it the master and not the servant of the purpose for which it was designed – namely, to ascertain the meaning of the parties from the words they have used ... Moreover, the main argument of construction which justifies the application of the rule does not apply in commercial documents. It is that if the general words have an unrestricted meaning the enumerated items are surplusage. The presumption against surplusage is of little value in ascertaining the intention of the parties in commercial documents, as many great judges have recognised. In *Burrell and Sons v F Green and Co* [1914] 1 KB 293 Bailhache J said that he was unimpressed with the argument of redundancy 'because charterparties contain many redundant words'.

(d) Wills

The *ejusdem generis* rule will be overridden by the presumption that a person who makes a will does not intend to die intestate as to any part of his property and, therefore, the will must be construed to prevent that result. See *Bridges v Bridges* (1729) 2 Eq Cas Abr 330.

6.7.3   The rule is not a cure for poor drafting

The *ejusdem generis* rule is intended to guard against accidental omissions and it cannot be a cure for poor or inadequate drafting. If a clause is drafted without considering all the events which it may be needed to cover, or fails to set out a sufficiently wide class or genus in relation to the wider general words, or the wider general words are not wide enough, the rule will not avoid these inadequacies. Several decided cases illustrate the difficulties which can arise. In *Tillmanns and Co v SS Knutsford Co* [1908] AC 406, a bill of lading provided that there would be no liability for failure to deliver a cargo at a port if it was, in the opinion of the master of the ship, unsafe to do so 'in consequence of war, disturbance or any other cause'. The master failed to deliver cargo at a port because it was ice bound. This was held to be a breach of contract because failure to deliver to a port which was ice bound did not fall under the clause. The words 'any other cause' had to be construed *ejusdem generis* with 'war, disturbance', as these referred to violent acts caused by man rather than acts of nature.

In *Fenwick v Schmalz* (1868) LR 3 CP 313, a charterparty required the defendant to load the plaintiff's ship with coal 'except in cases of riots, strikes or any other accidents'. The defendant failed to load the ship because of a snowstorm. The defendant was unable to rely on the clause because a snowstorm was not within the preceding genus which referred to violent acts of man – and it could not fall within the general words 'any other accidents' as it could not be described as an accident, but was a natural occurrence.

6.7.4   Dangers of examples

If a clause contains general words which either include or exclude something from its effect, there may be a temptation to add examples after the general words by way of illustration. Unless it is clear that the items referred to are only by way of example, the *ejusdem generis* rule may restrict the general words used in a way which was unintended. This problem was referred to by Scott LJ in *Beaumont-Thomas v Blue Star Line* (1939) 3 All ER 127 as:

> ... the common and pernicious practice of cramming a contract with particular illustrations of some general stipulation, which in a legal sense are wholly unnecessary, and just because they are unnecessary often afford a pretext for limiting general words in a way that was never intended.

In *Schloss Brothers v Stevens* [1906] 2 KB 665, Walton J referred to the same problem:

> It was said for the defendant that, if all risks were covered, why refer specially to risks of robbery with or without violence, negligence, etc? On the other hand, it is very common to find in such contracts, although perfectly general words are made use of, including practically all risks, special reference to particular perils to which it is desired to draw special attention.

6.7.5   Excluding the rule

Since the *ejusdem generis* rule can cause difficulties, it is advisable to avoid its possible application. There are several drafting devices which may be used to indicate that it is not to apply. In *Chandris v Isbrandsen-Moller Co Inc* [1951] 1 KB 240, Devlin J referred to some of these. He said:

> Legal draftsmen are all familiar with the existence of the rule, and familiar too with the proper signals to hoist if they do not want it to apply. Phrases such as 'whether or not similar to the foregoing' and 'without prejudice to the generality of the foregoing' are often employed in legal draftership; and if the drafter has read the report of *Larsen v Sylvester and Co* [1908] AC 295 he will know that the addition of 'whatsoever' generally serves the same purpose. Commercial draftsmen are not usually taught these rules.

Another method of excluding the rule is by setting out the class or genus in exhaustive terms, as indicated above.

6.8   Enumerations

6.8.1   Avoid enumerations

Enumerations of particulars should be avoided in drafting, even where the *ejusdem generis* rule is not applicable. It is difficult in many circumstances to make an exhaustive list of items, and, where this is possible, there is always the danger of accidental omission. Where an attempt is made to enumerate, an omission may be interpreted as deliberate exclusion under the maxim *expressio unius exclusio alterius* (that is, to express one thing is to impliedly exclude another). As Wills J said, in *Colquhoun v Brooks* (1887) 19 QBD 400:

> ... the maxim *expressio unius exclusio alterius* is one that certainly requires to be watched ... The failure to make the '*expressio*' complete very often arises from accident, very often from the fact that it never struck the drafter that the thing supposed to be excluded needed specific mention of any kind ...

6.8.2   Illustration

The following example illustrates the problems which can arise where an enumeration is incomplete, and how these can be avoided. A bequest in the will by a testatrix which is intended to dispose of her jewellery might be in the following terms:

> My watches, rings, necklaces and bracelets to my daughter, Ann.

If the list of items is exhaustive of the jewellery possessed by the testatrix, the bequest will have achieved its objective. But, if the testatrix also possessed several pairs of earrings, these may be taken to be excluded from the bequest, as would other jewellery such as hatpins, hairpins or tiaras. To avoid accidental omission, the safer course is to draft the bequest as:

> All my jewellery to my daughter, Ann.

If the testatrix insisted that certain items should be listed as a matter of caution because she regarded them as her most important pieces of jewellery, the bequest could be drafted as:

> All my jewellery including, but not restricted to, my watches, rings, necklaces and bracelets to my daughter, Ann.

In this case, the *ejusdem generis* rule is a potential danger, and the clause should not to be drafted as:

> My watches, rings, necklaces, bracelets and other jewellery to my daughter, Ann.

6.9   Two provisions in one sentence

Sometimes, a sentence or clause is drafted so that it contains two provisions. For example:

> I devise and bequeath all my real and personal property to my son, John.

In this clause, 'devise' is applicable only to real property and 'bequeath' is applicable only to personal property. The clause will be construed in this way under the maxim *reddendo singula singulis* (that is, render each to each). Thus, the clause will be read as if it were 'I devise all my real property to my son, John' and 'I bequeath all my personal property to my son, John'.

The use of this technique in drafting is not objectionable if it is possible for the reader to relate the relevant provisions to each other. However, it is likely that sentences or clauses which combine several provisions will be difficult for the reader to follow, and should be avoided. For example:

> The Employers and the Members of the Plan shall pay contributions to the Plan of 10% and 5% of Salary.

This clause is from the rules of a company pension plan. Under the maxim *reddendo singula singulis,* it is possible to conclude that the Employer's contributions are 10% and Members' contributions are 5%. The lay reader to whom the clause is intended to give information might not reach this conclusion. The clause would be better if redrafted as two clauses which state:

The Employer shall pay contributions of 10% of the Salary of each Member of the Plan.

Each Member shall pay contributions of 5% of Salary to the Plan.

CHAPTER

7

The Use of Particular Words

Words are the lawyer's tools of trade.

Lord Denning
The Discipline of Law (1979)

7.1 Introduction

The courts have, from time to time, pronounced on the effect of particular words in legal documents. Unfortunately, many legal documents continue to be drafted in a manner which suggests that no account has been taken of these decisions. This chapter is concerned with the legal effect of certain words which are frequently used in drafting legal documents, as well as some of the difficulties they can cause and how these might be avoided.

7.2 Use of 'shall'

7.2.1 Use 'shall' in the imperative sense

'Shall' should be used only in the imperative sense in a legal document to impose a duty or obligation on the legal subject to whom it refers. As is indicated below, 'shall' is sometimes used in legal documents in other ways, which should be avoided in the interests of clarity. As Coode said of 'shall':

> ... it denotes the compulsion, the obligation to act, (*scealan*, to owe, to be obliged) and does not prophesy that the party will or will not at some future time do the act. 'Thou shalt not do murder' is not a prediction, but the 'shalt' is obligatory in the present tense, continuously through all the time of the operation of the law.

'Shall' is used in the imperative sense in the following examples:

> The Trustees shall pay the sum of £100,000 to my son, John, on attaining the age of 21.

The tenant shall not sub-let the whole or a part of the premises.

The Purchaser shall pay to the Vendor on 1 March 2001 the sum of £25,000.

Employees shall pay 7% of their Pensionable Salary to the Pension Fund.

The Company shall at the request of ...

In these examples, 'shall' compels the person towards whom it is directed to discharge the duty or obligation.

7.2.2   Use of 'shall' in a directory sense

'Shall' is sometimes used in legal documents in a directory sense rather than an imperative sense to signify that some step must be taken if a right or option is to be exercised. The use of 'shall' in this sense ought to be avoided and alternative expressions sometimes used to indicate the directory nature of the provision. For example:

Notice of an appeal shall be filed within 21 days.

The use of 'shall' in this clause does not compel an appellant to file a notice of appeal, it is a direction to file a notice of appeal within 21 days if an appeal is to proceed. The use of 'shall' in the directory sense can be avoided in drafting, and the example above could be redrafted as:

Notice of an appeal must be filed within 21 days.

Or:

An appeal may be made by filing a notice of appeal within 21 days.

If 'shall' is used in both the imperative and the directory sense in the same document, it may be difficult to determine whether, in a given instance, it is used to signify a duty or obligation, or intended to be directory or imply futurity. The use of 'shall' in statutory provisions has often led to difficulty in this respect. In *Wallersteiner v Moir* [1974] 1 WLR 991, the Court of Appeal had to decide whether 'shall' as used in RSC Ord 19 r 7(1) was mandatory or directory. This provision set out the consequences for a defendant who failed to serve a defence in time and it permitted the plaintiff to apply to the court for judgment. It went on to state:

> On the hearing of the application the court shall give such judgment as the plaintiff appears entitled to on his statement of claim.

Despite persuasive arguments to the contrary, it was held that 'shall' was used in the directory sense and that the court was not required to give judgment for the plaintiff, but could refuse the plaintiff judgment if it considered for any reason that an injustice might be done by giving him judgment.

If 'shall' is used in the imperative sense only, the danger of confusion arising because it is used in both senses at the same time is likely to be avoided. This happened in *Cooke v New River Co* (1888) 38 Ch D 56. This case was concerned with the construction of a private Act of Parliament, which provided that a water company:

> ... shall, at the request of any consumer of water for purposes other than the purposes for or in respect of which the rates or charges are hereinbefore provided or limited, or at their own instance, afford a supply of water by means of a meter ...

'Shall' in this context was held to be both compulsory and directory. As Bowen LJ stated:

> It seems to me that the word 'shall' is compulsory when it is dealing with the action of the company set in motion at the request of the consumer, but that when it passes to the act of the company upon its own initiative it takes a colour from the words 'at their own instance' which give to the word 'shall', not altogether inappropriately, the meaning of 'may'.

Other examples of the use of 'shall' in a directory sense are:

> Cheques shall be made payable to ...

> Employees' contributions shall be deducted from their earnings and paid to ...

7.2.3   Use of 'shall' to imply futurity

'Shall' can be used to indicate that something is to be done if or when something else 'shall' happen in the future. In drafting legal documents, the use of 'shall' in this way should be avoided. This can be achieved by drafting in the present tense (see above, 6.3). An example of the use of 'shall' in the future tense is:

> I hereby covenant to settle upon the said trusts any property which
> I shall inherit under the will of my father.

In this example, 'shall' is not necessary and the clause would be equally effective if it were omitted. Other examples of the use of 'shall' in the future tense are:

> If any balance shall be due ...

> If the tenant shall give 28 days' notice to the landlord he may ...

In each of these examples, a switch to the present tense will avoid the need for 'shall', and they could be drafted as:

> If any balance is due ...

> If the tenant gives 28 days' notice to the landlord he may ...

In some old legal documents, 'shall' was used to imply futurity, so that events that had happened before the date on which the document was executed were excluded from the scope of the document. For example, if a settlor covenanted 'to settle all real property which I shall become possessed of or entitled to', the covenant would not include property which the settlor had become possessed of, or entitled to, before the date of the covenant (see *Wilton v Colvin* (1854) 23 LJ Ch 850). The use of 'shall' in this way is avoidable, so that, in the example given, it may be avoided by drafting the covenant as:

> ... to settle all real property which I become entitled to or possessed
> of after the date of this deed.

7.2.4 Use of 'shall' in different senses in the same provision

'Shall' should not be used in different senses in the same provision, as this may lead to confusion. For example:

> I leave my residuary estate to my sons in equal shares but if any son shall predecease me my executors shall pay his share to my sister, Mary.

In this example, the first use of 'shall' implies futurity, whilst the second use of 'shall' is in the form of a direction. The use of 'shall' in different senses in the same provision is avoidable, and where it occurs it is unlikely to be conducive to clarity. This clause could be redrafted so that 'shall' is used once only and in the imperative sense:

> I leave my residuary estate to my sons in equal shares and if any son predeceases me my executors shall pay his share to my sister, Mary.

7.2.5 Misuse of 'shall'

'Shall' is often used in legal documents in a way which is inappropriate. There are three instances where this can arise.

(a) In conferring rights or benefits

Provisions conferring rights or benefits sometimes state that a person 'shall' enjoy that right or benefit. The use of 'shall' in this way suggests that the person is *compelled* to enjoy the benefit. Thus, for example:

> The Employee shall receive a salary of £50,000 per annum.

> The copyright owner shall receive royalties of 15% of the price of each copy sold.

It would be possible to draft both examples without the use of 'shall' and indicate that a right or benefit is being conferred:

> The Employee will receive a salary of £50,000 per annum.

> The copyright owner will receive royalties of 15% of the price of each copy sold.

Or:

> The Employee is entitled to receive salary of £50,000 per annum.

> The copyright owner is entitled to receive royalties of 15% of the price of each copy sold.

(b) In definitions

Sometimes, definitions are couched in terms where 'shall' follows the word or term being defined. For example:

> 'Trustees' shall mean ...

> 'Value Added Tax' shall mean ...

Definitions are intended to be declaratory of the meaning of a word or term and there is little point in using 'shall', since it adds nothing. In modern statutes, 'shall' is not used in definitions (although it can be found in the definitions in some old statutes). There is little point in adding to the length of a document by inserting 'shall' in definitions, and the examples above would be equally effective if drafted as:

> 'Trustees' means ...

> 'Value Added Tax' means ...

(b) Negative subjects

'Shall' is sometimes used with a negative subject and it is advisable to avoid its use in this context. For example:

> No Trustee shall be liable for any loss of or any depreciation in or default upon any of the investments of the Trust Fund.

> No Employee shall ...

These might be redrafted without 'shall', as follows:

> The Trustees will not be liable for any loss of or any depreciation in or default upon any of the investments of the Trust Fund.

> No Employee may ...

Or:

> A Trustee is not liable for any loss of or any depreciation in or default upon any of the investments of the Trust Fund.

> An Employee may not ...

7.2.6 Alternatives to 'shall'

The use of 'shall' is sometimes regarded as rather too formal for certain types of legal document, especially those which deal with the rights and duties of consumers. In these cases, 'must' is often used in place of 'shall' to indicate an obligation. For example:

> You must give 28 days' notice in writing to terminate the agreement.

> You must not sub-let the house in any way.

7.3 Use of 'may'

7.3.1 'May' indicates a discretion

'May' should be used in a legal document to indicate that a right, power or privilege is being conferred. Case law indicates that, where 'may' is used, the person to whom it relates is given a discretion as to whether something should or should not be done. Thus, in *Re Baker* (1890) 44 Ch D 262, Cotton LJ observed:

> In my opinion there is given by the word 'may' a power the exercise of which there is a discretion.

The use of 'may' in the following examples imports a discretion:

> My Trustees may appoint the Trust Property to such of my children as they think fit and in default of appointment ...

> My Trustees may delegate all or any of their powers ...

7.3.2 'May' as obligatory

Although 'may' is generally construed as discretionary, case law indicates that it can, in an appropriate context, be construed as imposing an obligation rather than a discretion. For example, in *Re Shuter* [1960] 1 QB 142, 'may' was construed as obligatory in s 7 of the Fugitive Offenders Act 1881. This section enabled a fugitive in custody to make an application to the court to be discharged from custody. It stated:

> A superior court, upon application by or on behalf of the fugitive ... may, unless sufficient cause is shown to the contrary, order the fugitive to be discharged out of custody.

Lord Parker CJ concluded that, in the context, 'may' was mandatory because:

> ... if the discretion is completely at large and 'may' means 'may', then it would be quite unnecessary to have the words, 'unless sufficient cause is shown to the contrary'. Secondly, this is a case where what is sufficient cause in any particular case may well depend upon opinion and discretion. I think the natural meaning is 'shall' unless sufficient cause is shown to the contrary to order the fugitive to be discharged out of custody.

In *Entwistle v Dent* (1848) 1 Exch 812, 'may' was construed as 'must' in a letter from a London merchant to his agent in China. The letter stated:

> If tea is not obtainable at our limits you may invest one half of the whole proceeds in silk ...

The context in which these words appeared in the letter inferred that the agents were directed to invest in silk and did not have any discretion in the matter.

7.3.3 Ensuring that 'may' is discretionary

Since there is a danger that, in an appropriate context, 'may' could be construed as imposing an obligation, it is advisable in conferring a discretion to use additional words which will leave no doubt that a discretion is intended. Thus, in drafting rights and powers, the following formula might be adopted:

The Trustees may in their discretion pay ...

Or:

The Trustees may in their absolute discretion pay ...

Or:

The Trustees may if they think fit ...

Whether 'absolute' is added in the second of these examples is a matter of taste, but in each case there can be no doubt that a discretion is intended.

7.3.4   Other terms conferring discretions

Although 'may' is widely used to indicate that a power or discretion is being conferred, other words and terms can be used to do so, but it is suggested that they are avoided. They include:

- 'empowered'

    My trustees are empowered to ...

- 'shall have power'

    The use of this expression is better avoided. As indicated above, 7.2.3, the use of 'shall' in this way implies futurity and is unnecessary, as the following example illustrates:

    My Executors shall have power to ...

    This should be redrafted as:

    My Executors may in their discretion ...

- 'it shall be lawful'

    In *Julius v Oxford* (Bishop) (1880) 5 App Cas 214, Lord Cairns LC said of these words:

    The words 'it shall be lawful' are not equivocal. They are plain and unambiguous. They are words making that legal and possible which there would otherwise be no right or authority to do. They confer a faculty or power, and they do not of themselves do more than confer a faculty or power.

- 'it shall and may be lawful'

This expression, despite using 'shall', has been held in some cases to indicate a discretion rather than an obligation. Thus, in *Re Newport Bridge* (1859) 29 LJ MC 52, they were held to indicate a discretionary power. The use of 'it shall and may be lawful' is inadvisable in conferring a power, since the context in which it is used may indicate that an obligation is intended. In addition, it may be confused with expressions which have been held to import an obligation.

- 'shall and lawfully may'

In *Chapman v Milvain* (1852) 5 Ex 61, Parke B said:

> The words 'shall and lawfully may' are in their import obligatory, and ought according to established rule, to have that construction unless it would lead to some absurd or inconvenient consequence ...

- 'shall and may'

This expression has caused much trouble and ought to be avoided. In some instances, it has been held to be discretionary and, in others, obligatory. In *Re Lamb* (1888) 32 SJ 680, it was said they might be discretionary. However, in *Re Burton and Blinkhorn* [1903] 2 KB 300, Wills J said of *Re Lamb*:

> I observe that, although the members of the Court of Appeal said the effect of those words is that there is, or may be, a discretion, no one has given any reason for it, or explained why the word 'shall' ceases to be obligatory, merely because it is followed by 'and may'.

7.3.5 'May' to indicate futurity

Although 'may' is normally used to confer a right or power it may, in an appropriate context, denote futurity. For example:

I guarantee any balance that may be due ...

I leave my residuary estate to my children in equal shares provided that the share of any child who may die in my lifetime shall be divided equally between my grandchildren.

'May' as used in the first example refers to a future balance; in the second example it refers to a contingency. If, as indicated above, 6.3, the document is drafted in the present tense, the need to use 'may' in these cases is avoidable, so that the examples above could be redrafted as:

I guarantee any balance that is due ...

I leave my residuary estate to my children in equal shares provided that the share of any child who dies in my lifetime shall be divided equally between my grandchildren.

7.4   Use of 'and' and 'or'

7.4.1   Introduction

The connectives 'and' and 'or' have caused many difficulties in the construction of legal documents, witnessed by the large number of reported cases, especially in relation to wills and charities in which their effect was in dispute. These cases demonstrate the need for care in their use. This section is concerned with some of the considerations which should be borne in mind in using them.

7.4.2   General rules

- 'And' is conjunctive

  'And' unites the words or clauses which precede and follow it. For example, a disposition in a will of 'all my sons and daughters in equal shares' includes all persons who are the testator's sons or his daughters. 'And' is frequently used in legal drafting with conjunctive effect to set out conditions and, where it is used in this way, all conditions linked by it must be fulfilled. For example:

> If my son, X, dies before me and is not survived by children or issue ...

> 'Sale Shares' means all the shares in the capital of the company allotted and in issue at the date hereof.

The use of 'and' to link conditions is clearly seen in clauses which are paragraphed, as in the following example taken from a share purchase agreement:

> The company:
>
> (a) is registered for the purposes of VAT; and
>
> (b) has complied fully with the legislation relating to VAT; and
>
> (c) has never been treated as a member of a group of companies for the purposes of VAT legislation; and
>
> (d) has maintained full and complete records as are appropriate or requisite for the purposes of VAT legislation; and
>
> (e) has not been required by the Commissioners of Customs and Excise to give security for the purposes of VAT legislation.

- 'Or' is disjunctive and introduces an alternative

In legal documents, 'or' is generally treated as indicating that the matters which precede and follow it are alternatives. In *Re Diplock* [1941] Ch 253, a testator left the residue of his property to his executors 'for such charitable institution or institutions or other charitable or benevolent object or objects in England as my acting executor or executors may, in their absolute discretion select'. Greene MR said:

> ... it does not seem to me to be open to doubt that the testator is giving to his trustees an option to apply his residue either first, to a charitable institution or institutions, or, secondly, to some other charitable object, or thirdly, to some benevolent object or objects. The word 'or' is *prima facie*, and in the absence of some restraining context, to be read as disjunctive, and if a testator wishes to give his trustees a discretion to apply his property either to charitable or to benevolent objects,

> I do not myself know what word in the English language he can more suitably use than the word 'or'.

Other examples illustrating the disjunctive when 'or' is used are:

> For such of my children as attain the age of 18 years or marry under that age ...

> The purchaser or his agents ...

- 'And' is inclusive

For example, if a contract states that, in the event of a breach by the seller,

> ... the buyer may rescind and claim damages,

the effect of 'and' is to give the buyer the choice of (a) rescinding; (b) claiming damages; or (c) rescinding and claiming damages.

- 'Or' is usually exclusive, but may be inclusive

'Or' is usually interpreted as exclusive, so that it calls for a choice between the matters which it links – for example, 'black or white coffee'. In some circumstances, it may interpreted as inclusive, and both of the matters that it links can be fulfilled. It seems that 'or' is likely to be treated as inclusive unless the concepts it links are mutually exclusive. For example:

> The seller may retain or sell the goods.

It is impossible for the seller to both retain and sell the goods, so he has the choice of (a) retaining or (b) selling. If the concepts are not mutually exclusive, 'or' can be inclusive. For example, a gift in a will for 'charitable or benevolent objects', as *Re Diplock* (above) indicates, enables the executors of the will to apply the gift for charitable or benevolent purposes, or both. Thus, if the example 'the buyer may rescind and claim damages' were drafted as:

> ... the buyer may rescind or claim damages,

the effect would be to give the buyer the choice of (a) rescinding, or (b) claiming damages; or, it seems, (c) rescinding and claiming damages. In the last example, it is not entirely clear that the use of 'or' gives the buyer the right to both rescission and damages, and to eliminate this uncertainty the clause could be redrafted as 'the buyer may rescind or claim damages or both'. As will be indicated below, 7.5, the clause should not be drafted as 'the buyer may rescind and/or claim damages'.

7.4.3   'And' as 'or'

Where 'and' is used between the last two adjectives or nouns in a string of adjectives or nouns in a clause, its function is to complete the list. For example, 'doctors, dentists, lawyers, accountants and actuaries'. When 'and' is used for this purpose, each adjective or noun in the string of adjectives or nouns will be construed as independent or disjunctive so that there is a choice between the adjectives or nouns in the list. In *Re Eades* [1920] 2 Ch 353, a testator made a bequest for 'religious, charitable and philanthropic objects'. Sargant J observed that there were only two possible constructions: (a) that the objects must possess all three characteristics; or (b) that the objects need only have any one of the three characteristics. He went on:

> Such a construction as the second is sometimes referred to as a disjunctive construction, and as involving the change of the word 'and' into 'or'. This is a short and compendious way of expressing the result of the construction, but I doubt whether it indicates accurately the mental conception by which the result is reached. The conception is one, I think, which regards the word 'and' as used conjunctively and by way of addition, for the purpose of enlarging the number of objects within the area of selection; and it does not appear to be a false mental conception, or one really at variance with the ordinary use of language, merely because it involves in the result that the qualifications for selection are alternative or disjunctive. Further, the greater the number of the qualifications or characteristics enumerated, the more probable, as it seems to me, is a construction which regards them as multiplying the kinds or classes of objects within the area of selection, rather

than as multiplying the number of qualifications to be complied with, and so diminishing the objects within the area of selection.

In *AG for New Zealand v Brown* [1917] AC 393, 'and' was construed disjunctively where it was used both in relation to adjectives and nouns. The case concerned a will in which the residue was to be held by the trustees 'for such charitable benevolent, religious and educational institutions societies associations and objects as they in their uncontrolled discretion shall select'. The context of the will suggested a disjunctive interpretation.

7.4.4   'Or' as 'and'

'Or' may, in an appropriate context, be construed as 'and'. In *Re Hayden* [1931] 2 Ch 333, a testator left freehold property to a named person and directed that, after her death, it was to be divided equally between 'her sisters or their issue'. One sister had issue, but the others did not, and the will did not contain a provision that issue were to take the shares of their parents. Luxmoore J held that the context required that 'or' be construed as 'and' to make sense of the other words used in the will.

Although 'or' may be construed as 'and', it cannot in itself mean 'and'. As Jessel MR pointed out in *Morgan v Thomas* [1882] 9 QBD 643:

> You will find it said in some cases that 'or' means 'and'; but 'or' never does mean 'and' unless there is a context which shows it is used for 'and' by mistake. The instance I have given is this. Suppose a testator said, 'I give the black cow on which I usually ride to AB', and he usually rode on a black horse; of course the horse would pass but I do not think that any annotator of cases would put in the marginal note that 'cow' means 'horse'. You correct the wrong word used by the testator by the context; when you find that it was an animal on which he daily rode, you would say he meant a horse, he would not ride a cow in this country. It is not that the word has a different meaning from that which it usually bears, but the context usually shows the testator has by mistake used one word for another.

7.4.5   'And' may be joint or several

'And' may, depending on the context in which it is used, be either joint or several in its effect. For example:

> ... my residue to my nephews and nieces.

The use of 'and' to connect 'nephews' and 'nieces' is several, as every person who is a nephew or a niece of the testator is entitled to benefit. However, difficulties can arise if 'and' is used between nouns or adjectives which overlap. In these circumstances, it may be unclear whether 'and' was intended to be joint or several. For example:

> Every person who is a wife and a mother ...

Or:

> Every person who is a director and an employee of the company.

These provisions may be either joint or several. If they are construed as joint, the first will only apply to persons who are both wives and mothers, and the second will only apply to persons who are both directors and employees. If they are several, the first will apply to persons who are *either* wives or mothers and the second will apply to persons who are *either* directors or employees. The uncertainty could be avoided by the using express words to indicate the construction which is intended. For example:

> Every person who is both a wife and a mother ...

> Every person who is either a wife or a mother ...

And:

> Every person who is both a director and an employee of the company ...

> Every person who is either a director or an employee of the company.

7.5   Avoid 'and/or'

7.5.1   Do not use and/or

The expression 'and/or' should not be used in legal documents, as it puts together 'and', which is generally conjunctive, with 'or', which is generally disjunctive, and gives a provision an apparently contradictory effect. The use of 'and/or' seems to have developed as a shorthand method of stating 'A or B or both' so that it reads 'A and/or B'. Case law states that it can lead to unnecessary problems in construction, especially where it has been used thoughtlessly in the belief that it enables a provision to cover maximum ground with minimal use of words. These points should be sufficient to make its use out of bounds in legal drafting. However, it is not good English, and it has also attracted harsh judicial criticism in cases where the court has been asked to determine its meaning in a given context. In *Re Lewis* [1942] Ch 424, a will directed that the residue of the testator's estate should go to his wife for life, but if she predeceased him it directed 'all to Margaret Ann and/or John Richards'. Farwell J commented:

> The expression 'and/or' is unfortunate. I do not think I have met it before in a will, and I hope I shall never meet it again. I have, however, to put a meaning on it, if possible. Several cases have been cited which I do not think assist me. I have come to the conclusion that this gift is not void for uncertainty. I think that the testator meant that Margaret Ann and John Richards should take the residue as joint tenants but that if Margaret Ann did not survive the testator, the gift to John Richards was to take effect in substitution for the joint gift.

In this case, both Margaret Ann and John Richards survived the testator and the decision indicates the position if only John Richards had survived the testator. However, it is not clear how the provision would have been construed if only Margaret Ann Richards had survived the testator.

Viscount Simon LC was more forthright in his opinion of 'and/or' in *Bonitto v Fuerst Bros and Co Ltd* [1944] AC 75. In this case, paragraph 18 of a statement of claim contained a claim for a *quantum meruit* and used 'and/or' four times. This resulted in confusion in the pleadings and prompted a stinging comment:

> Paragraph 18 stated the alternative claim in a variety of phrases, separated from one another by the repeated use of that bastard conjunction 'and/or' which has, I fear, become the commercial court's contribution to basic English.

7.5.2 Problems arising from the use of 'and/or'

The main problem arising from using 'and/or' is that it does not indicate with sufficient precision the intended meaning behind a provision and this may eventually result in the provision being construed to have a meaning either wider or narrower that that actually intended. *Re Lewis* (cited above) provides an example in this respect. Other examples arise where 'and/or' is used to connect three or more objects, as in 'A, B and/or C', and where it is used more than once in the same sentence, as in 'A and/or B and/or C'. An example of the former is *Cuthbert v Cumming* (1855) 10 Exch 809, in which Alderson B was asked to construe a contract 'to load a full and complete cargo of sugar, molasses and/or any other lawful produce'. He held that, in the context, the obligation was to load either (a) sugar and molasses or other legal produce, or (b) sugar and molasses, or (c) other lawful produce. It will be noted that the obligation did not include loading either sugar or molasses alone. Thus A, B and/or C meant, in this context: (a) A, B and C; or (b) A and B; or (c) C, but not A alone or B alone. The use of 'and/or' more than once in the same provision is likely to cause real difficulties in construction, as in 'A and/or B and/or C'. This provision could have at least seven different meanings, namely: (a) A, B and C; or (b) A only; or (c) B only; or (d) C only; or (e) A and B; or (f) B and C; or (g) A and C. The context may in each case give some assistance in determining which one or more of these meanings is intended, but it is hardly a satisfactory method of determining the meaning of a provision.

7.6   Use of 'such'

7.6.1   Used to refer to nearest antecedent

'Such' is frequently used in legal documents to refer to a person or thing which has already been mentioned in order to avoid the need to refer again in full to that person or thing. As Kindersley VC said in *Stolworthy v Sancroft* (1864) 33 LJ Ch 708:

> Having described particular persons or things, a passage follows speaking of such persons and such things, meaning 'as aforesaid', referring to what has gone before.

'Such', if used in this way, secures an economy of words. For example:

> ... the asset register of the Company comprises a complete and accurate record of all plant and machinery vehicles and equipment owned used or possessed by the Company and such register is accurate in all respects.

The reference to 'such register' avoids the need to refer again to 'the asset register of the Company', which would be unnecessarily longwinded. The use of 'such register' will be regarded as referring back to its last antecedent. 'Such', when used in this way, avoids the danger of ambiguity which can arise if a pronoun is used to refer to the antecedent. For example:

> I leave Greenacre to my brother, James Smith, to hold upon trust for my son, John Smith, but if he dies before me I leave the same to my nephew, Richard Smith, to hold upon trust for my grandson, Peter Smith.

This clause leaves much to be desired. 'He' as used in this clause could refer to either James Smith or John Smith. It is likely that the testator intended to refer to John Smith, as he is the nearest antecedent to 'he'. However, there is potential ambiguity which could be avoided by the use of 'such'. The clause might be redrafted as:

> I leave Greenacre to my brother, James Smith, to hold upon trust
> for my son, John Smith, but if such son dies before me I leave the
> same to my nephew, Richard Smith, to hold upon trust for my
> grandson, Peter Smith.

'Such son' could be avoided altogether in this clause, if desired, by
references to 'my son' or 'my said son' or 'my son, John', depending
on the tastes of the drafter.

The use of 'such' can cause confusion if care is not taken to
ensure that it refers to an antecedent. This will happen if it is used
in a clause which does not have an antecedent to which it can
relate, or if there are several antecedents in other clauses to which
it could relate – for example, a clause in a will which refers to 'such
beneficiary' in which no beneficiary is otherwise referred to, but
where other clauses in the will refer to several named beneficiaries.

7.6.2   Unnecessary use of 'such'

'Such' is sometimes used in legal documents where it is
unnecessary and can easily be avoided without causing ambiguity.
It is often used unnecessarily as a demonstrative adjective or
demonstrative noun. For example:

> I leave my residuary estate to my executors to hold upon trust for
> my sister, Mary, for life and after her death for such of my children
> as should then be living, in such shares and in such proportions as
> my said sister, Mary, shall appoint and in default of appointment to
> my said children in equal shares.

'Such' is used three times. The first use could be avoided by using
'those', and it might be better to redraft 'for such of my children as
should then be living' as 'for my children then living'. The second
and third uses of 'such' are antiquated and could be replaced by
'the'. Other examples in which 'such' could be replaced by clearer
words are:

> The seller agrees to sell and the buyer agrees to buy the stock-in-
> trade of the business at Completion at such price, where the
> parties fail to agree, to be determined by such valuer appointed by

the parties and in default of such appointment by a valuer appointed under the Arbitration Act 1950.

'Such' is used three times, and in each case it is unnecessary and detracts from the clarity of the clause. The references to 'such price' and 'such valuer' could be redrafted as 'a price' and 'a valuer' and 'such appointment' would be adequate as 'appointment'. The clauses would then read:

> The seller agrees to sell and the buyer agrees to buy the stock-in-trade of the business at Completion at a price, where the parties fail to agree, to be determined by a valuer appointed by the parties and in default of appointment by a valuer appointed under the Arbitration Act 1950.

7.7   Use of 'same'

'Same' is often used as a pronoun in legal drafting instead of pronouns such as 'he' or 'she', 'him' or 'her', 'they or 'them' or 'it'. Its use as a pronoun, as Fowler's *Modern English Usage* points out, 'was once good English, abundant in the Bible and the Prayer Book, but is now an archaism surviving mainly in legal documents and commercialese'. The continued use of 'same' as a pronoun in legal documents is avoidable and, consequently, difficult to justify when alternative pronouns can be used which result in greater clarity without affecting precision. In the following examples, 'same' is avoidable:

> I devise my freehold land at Barnhill, Middlesex to my trustees upon trust to sell the same and hold the net proceeds of sale and the net rents and profits until sale upon the following trusts ...

In this example, 'same' could be replaced by 'it', or the clause could be amended so that the words 'to sell the same' are replaced by 'for sale', since there is nothing else mentioned in the clause which could be held on trust for sale. So, it would read:

> I devise my freehold land at Barnhill, Middlesex to my trustees upon trust for sale and hold the net proceeds of sale and the net rents and profits until sale upon the following trusts ...

Another example is drawn from a contract of employment:

> ... the company shall provide and maintain for the sole use of the employee while on business of the company a motor car of suitable type and shall pay all expenses in connection with such use of the same and the same shall be changed from time to time in accordance with the company's policy regarding vehicle replacements.

The use of 'same' twice in four consecutive words is avoidable, and there is considerable scope for other improvements. The clause might be redrafted to avoid the use of 'same', as follows:

> ... the company shall provide and maintain for the sole use of the employee while on business of the company a motor car of suitable type and shall pay all expenses in connection with such use of the motor car which shall be changed from time to time in accordance with the company's policy regarding vehicle replacements.

7.8   Use of 'said'

'Said' is used liberally in some legal documents when this is either unnecessary or avoidable. The only purpose 'said' can have in a legal document is to refer back to some person or thing already mentioned, as in the case of 'such'. In *Shepherd's Trustees v Shepherd* [1945] SC 60, Lord Normand said:

> In following as you read it any document, when you come upon a word such as the 'said' or 'such' containing a reference to an earlier part of the document and to some person or thing already mentioned, you do not begin by re-reading the document from the beginning; you look backwards, and you take the nearest sensible antecedent as the appropriate antecedent for the word of reference.

The use of 'said', or its counterpart, 'aforesaid', is avoidable legal jargon, and can and should be eliminated. Its use to refer back to something already mentioned does not assist clarity and can give a document a turgid appearance. The following considerations may assist in removing 'said' and 'aforesaid' from a document:

- Frequent use of 'said' and 'aforesaid' may indicate that the person or thing which is prefixed with them should have been defined in the document. For example, if a settlement makes frequent reference to the settlor as 'the said John Smith' or 'the said settlor John Smith', it would be better to define John Smith as 'the settlor' in order to cut out a lot of unnecessary verbiage.

- 'Said' and 'aforesaid' are also used as a prefix in references to a person or thing where it would not be appropriate to define that person or thing. In such cases, their use is unnecessary, since the proper description of the person or thing is not enhanced by them. In such cases, their use is often little more than a bad habit which, in some instances, may lead to absurdity. For example, a reference in a will to 'my said wife, Mary' is silly, since it implies that the testator has more than one wife; 'my wife Mary' would be adequate.

- 'Said' and 'aforesaid' are sometimes used to refer in a general way to a provision in another part of the same document. For example:

    Any agent appointed as aforesaid may ...

Or:

    The trustees shall invest the income as aforesaid ...

These references are potentially uncertain, and they should be amended so that reference is made to the clause in which the provision referred to is contained:

    Any agent appointed under clause 6 may ...

Or:

    The trustees shall invest the income in accordance with clause 5 ...

7.9   Use of 'between' and 'among'

There is a rule of grammar that 'between' must be used only with reference to the relationship between two persons or things and that, if there are more than two, 'among' is the correct preposition.

The *Oxford English Dictionary* warns against this as a superstition and points out that 'between' has long been used to express the relation of a thing to many surrounding things severally and individually, and that 'among' expresses a relation to them collectively and vaguely. On this basis, 'between' would be appropriate in both of the following examples:

> £10,000 to be divided equally between A and B.

> £10,000 to be divided equally between A, B, C and D.

'Among' would not be a suitable replacement for 'between' in either of these examples. The instances where 'among' will be appropriate in drafting are likely to be few. For example, it would be appropriate in the following bequest:

> I leave my residuary estate to my trustees to divide among such charitable objects as they shall in their absolute discretion select.

'Between' and 'among' are frequently used in drafting dispositions in wills. Although, as indicated, 'between' will normally be the most appropriate preposition, its use may not always result in the required precision in drafting. For example:

> My trustees shall hold my residuary estate on trust to divide the same between my son, X and the children of my son, Y.

If Y has two daughters, A and B, the clause might be construed in two ways. First, it might be construed as giving a half share of the residuary estate to X and a half share of the residuary estate to A and B, that is, one-quarter each. Secondly, it might be construed as giving one-third shares of the residuary estate to each of X, A and B. The clause should be redrafted to eliminate this uncertainty and, if the first construction is intended, it could be expressed as:

> My residuary estate to my trustees to hold one-half for my son, X and one-half for the children of my son, Y.

Or, if A and B are the only children of Y:

> My residuary estate to my trustees to hold one-half for my son, X, one-quarter for my granddaughter, A, and one-quarter for my granddaughter, B.

If the second interpretation of the clause is intended, it could be drafted as:

> My residuary estate to my trustees to hold one-third for my son X, one-third for my granddaughter, A and one-third for my granddaughter, B.

Or:

> My residuary estate to my trustees to hold in equal shares for my son X, my granddaughter, A and my granddaughter, B.

7.10   Use of 'where' and 'when'

'Where' and 'when' are commonly used in legal documents to indicate the circumstances in which a provision is to operate. Sometimes they are used incorrectly. As a general rule, 'where' should be used if it is contemplated that the circumstances in which the provision will operate will occur frequently, and 'when' should be used if it is contemplated that the provision will operate only once. If a clause begins with 'where' or 'when', it should be apparent from the words which follow whether it is intended to apply to circumstances which will occur frequently or occur only once. For example:

> Where the employer has required a contractor to provide a driver for a motor vehicle or a heavy goods vehicle the contractor shall ensure that such driver is the holder of a current licence to drive a motor vehicle or a current licence to drive a heavy goods vehicle of that type or class of heavy goods vehicle.

> When the borrower repays the lender the Principal Sum together with any interest outstanding on the Principal Sum up to the date of payment of the Principal Sum, the lender covenants with the borrower at the request and the cost of the borrower, to execute a statutory discharge or a reconveyance of the property.

Sometimes, 'where' or when' are misused within a clause. For example:

> Where my son attains the age of 21 years the trustees shall pay him the sum of £100,000.

As the settlor's son will attain 21 on one occasion only, 'where' is inappropriate and 'when' should have been used. Similarly, if a document refers to events such as death or the termination of a contract, these should be preceded by 'when'. For example:

> When my widow dies my estate shall pass to ...

Or:

> When the term under this lease expires ...

7.11   Use of 'if'

'If' usually precedes a condition. For example:

> I leave my residuary estate to my wife, Mary, but if she predeceases me I leave it to my son, James, absolutely.

Or:

> If a trustee resigns or retires or dies the settlor shall appoint a new trustee in his place.

Or:

> If we do not receive full payment for your order as required under clause 3.3 delivery will be delayed until full payment is made and another delivery date is agreed with you.

In legislative drafting, conditions are expressed in the present indicative regardless of whether they are conditions precedent, present or subsequent. This rule is not always followed in drafting legal documents, especially in drafting of wills and trusts, where it would enable unnecessary words to be omitted and assist clarity. For example:

> If my son should die before me ...

There is no need to add 'should' and the provision could be redrafted in shorter and clearer terms as:

> If my son dies before me ...

Another example is:

> If there shall be no grandchildren of mine alive at my wife's death ...

If this is redrafted in the present indicative, it will be much clearer:

> If there are no grandchildren of mine alive at my wife's death ...

7.12   'Any', 'each' and 'every'

'Any', 'each' and 'every' are often used where 'a' or 'an' would be equally effective and clearer without any resulting loss of meaning. For example:

> Where any son of mine dies before me his share shall be divided equally between my surviving sons.

This could be redrafted as:

> Where a son of mine dies before me his share shall be divided equally between my surviving sons.

Similarly:

> Each person who is an employee of the Company and who has attained the age of 25 years may apply for membership of the Fund,

should be redrafted as:

> A person who is an employee of the Company and who has attained the age of 25 years may apply for membership of the Fund.

And:

> Every employee is entitled to apply for membership of the staff association,

should be redrafted as:

> An employee is entitled to apply for membership of the staff association.

The use of 'any', 'each' and 'every' should be confined to those circumstances where their use is essential.

7.13   'Whereas'

'Whereas' is often used to introduce recitals in a deed, even when the deed otherwise avoids archaic language. The following example is from the recitals of an agreement for the sale and purchase of shares:

WHEREAS:

(1)   The Vendor is the beneficial owner of the whole of the issued and allotted share capital in the Company.

(2)   The Vendor has agreed to sell and the Purchaser has agreed to buy all the issued shares in the Company on the terms and conditions hereinafter contained.

'WHEREAS' could be avoided by calling the recitals 'RECITALS'. Indeed, consideration should be given to whether recitals need to be inserted into a deed at all, or whether the contents of the recitals could be relegated to a schedule at the back of the document. They are normally used as a form of introduction in a deed to set out the background to the transaction which is evidenced by the deed. In many instances, this introduction is unnecessary and may be repeated in the operative part of the deed. In *Bath and Mountague's Case* (1693) 3 Ch Cas 55, Holt CJ said:

The reciting part of a deed is not at all a necessary part either in law or in equity. It may be made use of to explain a doubt of the intention and the meaning of the parties, but it hath no effect or operation.

Sometimes, 'WHEREAS' is inserted before each paragraph in the recitals. This is, fortunately, uncommon in modern legal documents and is quite unnecessary.

CHAPTER

8 Drafting Pleadings

*What is important is that the pleadings should make clear
the general nature of the case of the pleader ...*

McPhilemy v Times Newspapers
[1999] 3 All ER 775, per Lord Woolf MR

8.1 Introduction

The Civil Procedure Rules 1998 (CPR) are now in force. They have
replaced most of those parts of the Rules of the Supreme Court
and the County Court Rules, which relate to the drafting of the
documents which set out the case of parties to litigation. These
documents are now called 'statements of case'. They were
previously called 'pleadings'.

A primary objective of the CPR is to reduce the cost and
duration of litigation. There is a heavy emphasis on early disclosure
of evidence and witness statements, and under the CPR, the role of
statements of case will probably be smaller than the role of
pleadings under the old rules.

In *McPhilemy v Times Newspapers* [1999] 3 All ER 775, Lord
Woolf, the architect of the CPR, explained the role of 'pleadings' in
the light of the new rules. This was a defamation case, but the
explanation has general application. He said (pp 792–93):

> The need for extensive pleadings including particulars should be
> reduced by the requirement that witness statements are now
> exchanged. In the majority of proceedings identification of the
> documents upon which a party relies, together with copies of that
> party's witness statements, will make the detail of the nature of the
> case the other side has to meet obvious. This reduces the need for
> particulars in order to avoid being taken by surprise. This does not
> mean that pleadings are now superfluous. Pleadings are still
> required to mark out the parameters of the case that is being
> advanced by each party. In particular they are still critical to identify

the issues and the extent of the dispute between the parties. What is important is that the pleadings should make clear the general nature of the case of the pleader. This is true both under the old rules and the new rules. The Practice Direction to r 16 para 9.3 (*Practice Direction: Statements of Case,* CPR Pt 16) requires, in defamation proceedings, the facts on which a defendant relies to be given. No more than a *concise* statement of those facts is required.

As well as their expense, excessive particulars can achieve directly the opposite result from that which is intended. They can obscure the issues rather than providing clarification. In addition, after disclosure and the exchange of witness statements, pleadings frequently become of only historic interest ... [In the present case] the case is overburdened with particulars and simpler and shorter statements of case would have been sufficient. Unless there is some obvious purpose to be served by fighting over the precise terms of a pleading, contests over their terms are to be discouraged ... [Emphasis in original.]

So, although statements of case continue to be important, in future they are likely to be shorter (for fear that long statements of case might fall foul of the proportionality principle, and incur costs penalties), and technical points on pleadings (which paid many a junior barrister's gas bills and robbed many another of sleep) are likely to be discouraged. This does not mean that sloppiness is acceptable. Imprecise expression in pleadings is likely to obscure issues, run up costs and lead to judicial censure. But, the formalities which made the drafting of pleadings such a cabbalistic art are now either inessential or actively discouraged. Lord Woolf has made it clear that he dislikes Latin. The judges are increasingly disapproving of legalese in all its forms.

The CPR contain a number of detailed guidelines regarding the drafting of statements of case, which are intended to make it possible for non-legally qualified people to compete on equal terms with lawyers. Those guidelines are set out below. Wed those guidelines to the other principles of legal drafting, as detailed in the rest of this book, and you will produce coherent pleadings which no judge will get upset about.

This chapter is not a guide to civil procedure. It does not pretend to provide a comprehensive set of precedents. There are plenty of good books which do that.

8.2   Statements of case

8.2.1   General

The claim form (the equivalent of the old writ or County Court summons) must contain some details of the claim. There are two common types of fully pleaded statements of case: Particulars of Claim, and Defences. The Particulars of Claim set out the claimant's case. The Defence sets out the defendant's case.

Less often, there is a Reply. This is a claimant's response to issues raised in the Defence. By Pt 16.7 of the CPR, a claimant who does not file a reply shall not be taken to admit the matters raised in the Defence, but a claimant who opts to file a Reply but does not deal in it with something raised in the Defence is taken to require that thing to be proved. Always rare (and seriously endangered after the advent of the CPR) are statements of case subsequent to a Reply.

Commonly seen, too, are counterclaims (often forming part of a defence in a document headed 'Defence and Counterclaim'), and the claimant's response to a counterclaim (predictably, a 'Defence and Counterclaim'). It is very common for defendants to seek a contribution, indemnity or other remedy against other parties in the event of the defendant being found liable to the claimant. Where the party from whom a contribution or indemnity is sought is already a party to the litigation, there is automatic apportionment of liability between defendants, and there is technically no need for further documents claiming a contribution/indemnity, providing the defence sets out the nature of the claim. But, where the party from whom a contribution/indemnity is sought is not already a defendant, the defendant will serve a notice on that other party (who used to be called a third party), setting out the grounds on which the contribution/indemnity is sought. That notice used to be called a Third Party Notice. The third party might want to blame someone else. He used to do so by way of a Fourth Party Notice. And so on.

Under the CPR, all claims other than claims by a claimant against a defendant (which include counterclaims as well as claims by defendants against any party, whether or not already a party, for contribution, indemnity or some other remedy) are now governed by Pt 20 of the CPR, and parties other than the claimant and defendant are referred to as Part 20 parties, which tells the reader far less about their role in the litigation than the old 'third party', 'fourth party', etc, language.

Other documents which would previously have been classed as pleadings were requests for further and better particulars of a document, and replies to those requests. There is still provision for documents seeking clarification of, or further information in relation to, another party's case. That provision is in Pt 18 of the CPR, which makes it unnecessary to seek the information or clarification by means of a formal court document.

8.2.2 Contents

The CPR have changed things a lot. They give detailed directions about what should be in statements of case, and have also removed several prohibitions, such as the old prohibition against pleading evidence. The CPR insist on the principle of proportionality, which means that statements of case whose detail, and, therefore, cost, are disproportionate to the benefit conferred by the detail will be frowned on and are likely to be penalised by way of an order for costs. Any material in a statement of case which is an abuse of the process of the court, or which is otherwise likely to interfere with the just disposal of the case, is likely to be struck out: see Pt 3.4 of the CPR. But the CPR also insist on an early and definite clarification of issues. It is no longer possible to take refuge in vague traverses. Parties are under increasing pressure from extremely proactive judges wielding draconian case management powers to produce statements of case which say what the case actually is, in contrast to the old position, where pleadings often merely denied or refused or admit.

However, the legal profession has overestimated the effect of the new rules on statements of case. For example, contrary to apparently popular belief, there is no rule which says that a defendant cannot answer an allegation by saying that he does not admit it (intelligent and concise legal shorthand for 'I require the claimant to prove this allegation': the rules have not shifted the burden of proof). Because judges are not immune from popular belief, it might be wise to begin a document in which assertions are expressly 'not admitted' by a phrase like:

> Where, in this Defence, an assertion is expressed to be not admitted, the defendant does not know whether the assertion is true or false, and requires the claimant to prove the assertion.

The general provisions governing the contents of statements of case are in Pt 16 of the CPR. Annexed to Pt 16 is a Practice Direction which contains specific requirements for the contents of Particulars of Claim in personal injury, fatal accident, recovery of land and hire purchase claims, and for the contents of Defences in personal injury cases. Clause 14.3 of the Practice Direction contains permissive provisions which would have been anathema before the CPR. It says that a party may:

(1) refer in his statement of case to any point of law on which his claim or his defence, as the case may be, is based;

(2) give in his statement of case the name of any witness he proposes to call; and

(3) attach to or serve with his statement of case a copy of any document which he considers is necessary to his claim or defence, as the case may be (including any expert's report to be filed) ...

Each statement of case has to bear the title of the claim, including (as in the examples below) the name of the court, the claim number, the names of the parties and their role in the claim (for example, claimant, defendant, and so on), and the name of the document (for example, Particulars of Claim).

Individuals should be referred to by their full names (for example, Katie Sara Fawcett Paine). If the gender of the party is not clear from the name, the gender should be indicated by the word 'male' or 'female' in brackets afterwards.

Companies should be described in full and the company name followed by, in the case of public companies, 'public limited company' or 'plc' or, in the case of other companies, 'Limited' or 'Ltd'.

A partnership should be named with the words 'a firm' added after the name. An individual who carries on business under a trade name and sues or is sued in the course of his business should be referred to in person, with the trade name added. For example: 'John Smith (trading as 'Old Hat).'

Where a person under 18 is a party, that person is referred to as a child in the title, and must sue by a 'litigation friend' unless the court otherwise orders: see Pt 21 of the CPR. Thus, a claimant may be designated:

John Smith (a child, by his father and litigation friend Fred Smith).

If an action involves the estate of a deceased person, the estate should be represented by the executor or administrator of the estate, as appropriate.

8.3   The claim form

Part 16.2 of the CPR provides that:

(1)   The claim form must:

(a)   contain a concise statement of the nature of the claim;

(b)   specify the remedy which the claimant seeks;

(c)   where the claimant is making a claim for money, contain a statement of value ...;

(d)   contain such other matters as may be set out in a practice direction.

(2)   If the Particulars of Claim specified in rule 16.4 are not contained in, or are not served with the claim form, the claimant must state on the claim form that the Particulars of Claim will follow.

(3)   If the claimant is claiming in a representative capacity, the claim form must state what that capacity is.

(4)   If the defendant is sued in a representative capacity, the claim form must state what that capacity is ...

8.4   Particulars of Claim

8.4.1   General

Part 16.4 of the CPR provides that:

(1)   Particulars of Claim must include:

(a)   a concise statement of the facts on which the claimant relies;

(b)   if the claimant is seeking interest, a statement to that effect and the details set out in paragraph (2);

(c)   if the claimant is seeking aggravated damages or exemplary damages, a statement to that effect and his grounds for claiming them;

(d)   if the claimant is seeking provisional damages, a statement to that effect and his grounds for claiming them; and

(e)   such other matters as may be set out in a practice direction.

(2)   If the claimant is seeking interest he must:

(a)   state whether he is doing so

(i)   under the terms of a contract,

        (ii) under an enactment and if so which, or

        (iii) on some other basis and if so what that basis is; and

   (b) if the claim is for a specified amount of money, state

        (i)   the percentage rate at which interest is claimed,

        (ii) the date from which it is claimed,

        (iii) the date to which it is calculated, which must not be later than the date on which the claim form is issued,

        (iv) the total amount of interest claimed to the date of calculation, and

        (v) the daily rate at which interest accrues after that date.

The Practice Direction which accompanies Pt 16 contains directions about other matters, too. Clause 8 of the Practice Direction states:

8.1 Where a claim is made for an injunction or declaration in respect of or relating to any land or the possession, occupation, use or enjoyment of any land the particulars of claim must:

   (1) state whether or not the injunction or declaration relates to residential premises; and

   (2) identify the land (by reference to a plan where necessary).

8.2 Where a claim is brought to enforce a right to recover possession of goods the Particulars of Claim must contain a statement showing the value of goods.

8.3 ... [Not relevant in this context.]

8.4 Where a claim is based upon an oral agreement, the Particulars of Claim should set out the contractual words used and state by whom, to whom, when and where they were spoken.

8.5 Where a claim is based upon an agreement by conduct, the Particulars of Claim must specify the conduct relied on and state by whom, when and where the acts constituting the conduct were done.

8.6   In a claim in the High Court relating to a Consumer Credit Agreement, the Particulars of Claim must contain a statement that the action is not one to which s 141 of the Consumer Credit Act 1974 applies.

Clause 9 of the Practice Direction to Pt 16 details 'Matters which must be specifically set out in the Particulars of Claim if relied on'. It states:

9.1   A claimant who wishes to rely on evidence:

(1)   under s 11 of the Civil Evidence Act 1968 of a conviction of an offence; or

(2)   under s 12 of the above-mentioned Act of a finding or adjudication of adultery or paternity,

must include in his Particulars of Claim a statement to that effect and give the following details:

(1)   the type of conviction, finding or adjudication and its date;

(2)   the court or Court-Martial which made the conviction, finding or adjudication; and

(3)   the issue in the claim to which it relates.

9.2   The claimant must specifically set out the following matters in his Particulars of Claim where he wishes to rely on them in support of his claim:

(1)   any allegation of fraud;

(2)   the fact of any illegality;

(3)   details of any misrepresentation;

(4)   details of all breaches of trust;

(5)   notice or knowledge of a fact;

(6)   details of unsoundness of mind or undue influence;

(7)   details of wilful default;

(8)   any facts relating to mitigation of loss or damage.

Clause 10 of the Practice Direction to Pt 10 has further general provisions governing the contents of Particulars of Claim and other statements of case. It says:

10.1 Where a claim is for a sum of money expressed in a foreign currency it must expressly state:

   (1) that the claim is for payment in a specified foreign currency;

   (2) why it is for payment in that currency;

   (3) the Sterling equivalent of the sum at the date of the claim; and

   (4) the source of the exchange rate relied on to calculate the Sterling equivalent.

10.2 A subsequent statement of case must not contradict or be inconsistent with an earlier one; for example a reply to a defence must not bring in a new claim. Where new matters have come to light the appropriate course may be to seek the court's permission to amend the statement of case.

8.4.2 Personal injury claims: specific provisions

Clause 4 of the Practice Direction to Pt 16 of the CPR states that Particulars of Claim which relate to personal injury claims:

4.1 ... must contain:

   (1) the claimant's date of birth; and

   (2) brief details of the claimant's personal injuries.

4.2 The claimant must attach to his Particulars of Claim a schedule of details of any past and future expenses and losses which he claims.

4.3 Where the claimant is relying on the evidence of a medical practitioner the claimant must attach to or serve with his Particulars of Claim a report from a medical practitioner about the personal injuries which he alleges in his claim.

The clause goes on to make specific provisions about the details which must be provided where a claim for provisional damages is made.

8.4.3 Fatal accident claims: specific provisions

Clause 5 of the Practice Direction to Pt 16 states that Particulars of Claim which relate to fatal accident claims must state:

5.1 (1) that [the claim] is brought under the Fatal Accidents Act 1976;

(2) the dependants on whose behalf the claim is made;

(3) the date of birth of each dependant; and

(4) details of the dependency claim ...

and notes that bereavement damages can be claimed and a claim brought on behalf of the deceased's estate under the Law Reform (Miscellaneous Provisions) Act 1934.

8.4.4 Recovery of land and hire purchase claims

Clauses 6 and 7 of the Practice Direction to Pt 16 of the CPR contain detailed directions about what has to go in such Particulars of Claim, but these clauses are really summaries of what the substantive law in each type of case states is relevant, rather than procedural directions. They are designed as checklists which will help non-specialist litigants to avoid producing fatally defective Particulars of Claim.

8.5 Particulars of Claim: examples

8.5.1 Negligence: a running-down claim

IN THE CENTRAL LONDON COUNTY COURT   Claim No

BETWEEN

EDWARD CONFESSOR   *Claimant*

and

WILLIAM CONQUEROR   *Defendant*

PARTICULARS OF CLAIM

1. On 25 July 2000 the Claimant was crossing a pedestrian crossing near the main entrance to the Royal Courts of Justice, Strand, London WC2 when he was struck and knocked to the ground by a Triumph motor cycle registration number ABC 123 being driven by the Defendant.

2. The said accident was caused by the negligence of the Defendant.

PARTICULARS OF NEGLIGENCE

(a) Failing to give way to the Claimant on the pedestrian crossing.

(b) Failing to stop at the pedestrian crossing to permit the Claimant to cross.

(c) Failing to slow down on approaching the pedestrian crossing.

(d) Failing to notice the Claimant on the pedestrian crossing.

(e) Failing to keep any or any proper look out.

(f) Failing to stop, slow down steer or otherwise control his motor cycle so as to avoid hitting the Claimant.

(g) Driving too fast.

3. By reason of the said accident the Claimant, who was born on 21 July 1970, suffered pain and injury and sustained loss and damage.

PARTICULARS OF PERSONAL INJURIES

(a)   Multiple fractures to the right and left femurs.

(b)   Comminuted fracture of the left radius.

(c)   Bruising to the back and left hip.

(d)   He has undergone a total of eight surgical procedures in an effort to stabilise the femoral and radial fractures.

(e)   He has been left with a severe limp. He cannot walk more than 50 yards without using a stick.

(f)   He will have osteoarthritis in both hip joints by the time he is 40 years old. Probably he will need bilateral hip replacements by the age of 45.

(g)   Pronation and supination in his left wrist are greatly reduced. His grip strength is half what it should be.

(h)   As a result of the accident he lost his job as a nurse. He will never work again as a nurse or ever again doing anything but work which involves no walking, lifting or other physical exertion. He is currently unemployed, despite strenuous efforts to obtain work or training for alternative employment.

(i)   He claims for loss of congenial employment.

(j)   He is at a disadvantage on the labour market.

(k)   Further details are set out in the report of Mr Sawbones, Consultant Orthopaedic Surgeon, dated 23 January 2001, a copy of which is annexed hereto.

PARTICULARS OF SPECIAL DAMAGE

Particulars are set out in a separate Schedule annexed hereto.

4. Further the Claimant is entitled to and claims interest on the sum found due to him for such period and at such rate as the Court may think fit, pursuant to s 69 of the County Courts Act 1984.

AND the Claimant claims:

(1) damages;

(2) interest pursuant to statute as aforesaid.

K CANUTE

STATEMENT OF TRUTH

I .... believe that the facts stated in these Particulars of Claim are true.

Signed ....

DATED this   Day of   2001

8.5.2 A contract claim

IN THE CENTRAL LONDON COUNTY COURT   Claim No

QUEEN'S BENCH DIVISION

BETWEEN

LIONHEART LIMITED   *Claimant*

and

ETHELRED UNREADY LIMITED   *Defendant*

PARTICULARS OF CLAIM

1. (a) The Claimants are and were at all material times a company carrying on business as hoteliers.

   (b) The Defendants at all material times carried on business as electricians.

2. By a contract in writing dated 10 March 1993 made between the Claimants and the Defendants ('the contract'), the Defendants agreed to replace and update the entire electrical systems in the Claimants' hotel known as The Lionheart Inn, Norwich, in accordance with the specifications set out in Schedule One to the contract for the sum of £125,000.

3. By clause 3 of the contract it was expressly provided that the work should commence on 10 October 1993 and be completed on 10 December 1993.

4. Pursuant to clause 3 of the contract the Defendants began the said work on 10 October 1993.

5. In breach of clause 3 of the contract the Defendants did not complete the work until 15 March 1994.

6. By reason of the matters aforesaid the Claimants have suffered loss and damage.

PARTICULARS

Loss of profit:

(a) on hotel bar from 10 December 1993 to 15 March 1994: £45,000

(b) on hotel restaurants from 10 December 1993 to 15 March 1994: £65,000

(c) on hotel rooms from 10 December 1993 to 15 March 1994: £35,000

Advertising costs to preserve goodwill: £20,000

Total: **£165,000**

7. Further, the Claimants are entitled to and claim interest pursuant to s 69 of the County Courts Act 1984 on the amount found to be due to them at such rate and for such period as the Court thinks fit.

AND the Claimants claim:

(1) damages;

(2) interest pursuant to statute as aforesaid.

A GREAT

STATEMENT OF TRUTH

I .... believe that the facts stated in these Particulars of Claim are true.

Signed ....

DATED this   Day of   2001

8.6   The Defence

8.6.1   General

Part 16.5 deals with the contents of a Defence. It states:

(1)   In his Defence, the defendant must state:

    (a)   which of the allegations in the particulars of claim he denies;

    (b)   which allegations he is unable to admit or deny, but which he requires the claimant to prove; and

    (c)   which allegations he admits.

(2)   Where the defendant denies an allegation,

    (a)   he must state his reasons for doing so; and

    (b)   if he intends to put forward a different version of events from that given by the claimant, he must state his own version.

(3)   A defendant who

    (a)   fails to deal with an allegation, but

    (b)   has set out in his Defence the nature of his case in relation to the issue to which that allegation is relevant,

    shall be taken to require that allegation to be proved.

(4)   Where the claim includes a money claim, a defendant shall be taken to require that any allegation relating to the amount of money claimed be proved unless he expressly admits the allegation.

(5)   Subject to paragraphs (3) and (4), a defendant who fails to deal with an allegation shall be taken to admit that allegation.

(6)   If the defendant disputes the claimant's statement of value under rule 16.3 he must:

    (a)   state why he disputes it; and

    (b)   if he is able, give his own statement of the value of the claim.

(7) If the defendant is defending in a representative capacity, he must state what that capacity is ...

Part 16.6 is a permissive provision which allows a defendant to include in his Defence a defence of set off (a contention that he is entitled to money from the defendant and that he relies on this entitlement as a defence to the whole or part of the claim), whether or not that defendant is also making a Part 20 claim (a third or subsequent party claim) in relation to that money.

Clause 13 of the Practice Direction to Pt 16 requires a defendant to give details in his Defence of any limitation defence relied on.

A much discussed issue which relates particularly to the drafting of Defences is whether it is any longer permissible merely to say in respect of a particular assertion that that assertion is not admitted. As to this, see above, 3.2.

8.6.2 Personal injury claims: specific provisions

Clause 13 of the Practice Direction to Pt 16 sets out matters which must be dealt with in Defences in personal injury actions. It states:

13.1 Where the claim is for personal injuries and the claimant has attached a medical report in respect of his alleged injuries, the defendant should:

(1) state in his Defence whether he:

(a) agrees,

(b) disputes, or

(c) neither agrees nor disputes but has no knowledge of the matters contained in the medical report;

(2) where he disputes any part of the medical report, give in his defence his reasons for doing so; and

(3) where he has obtained his own medical report on which he intends to rely, attach it to his Defence.

13.2 Where the claim is for personal injuries and the claimant has included a schedule of past and future expenses and losses, the defendant should include in or attach to his Defence a counter-schedule stating:

(1) which of those items he:

  (a) agrees,

  (b) disputes, or

  (c) neither agrees nor disputes but has no knowledge of; and

(2) where any items are disputed, supplying alternative figures where appropriate.

8.6.3   Example: negligence: a running-down claim

The defendant's response to the particulars of claim above, 8.5.1, incorporating a counterclaim

IN THE CENTRAL LONDON COUNTY COURT   **Claim No**

BETWEEN:

EDWARD CONFESSOR   *Claimant*

and

WILLIAM CONQUEROR   *Defendant*

DEFENCE AND COUNTERCLAIM

DEFENCE

1. As to paragraph 1 of the Statement of Claim:

    (a)   It is averred, and insofar as therein pleaded admitted:

    (i) that at about 1.30 pm on 25 July 2000 the Defendant was riding his Triumph motorcycle, registration number ABC 123 ('the motorcycle') eastwards along the Strand, London WC2; and

    (ii) that on the east bound carriageway of the Strand, about 10 metres east of the pedestrian crossing opposite the main entrance of the Royal Courts of Justice, a collision occurred between the motorcycle and the Claimant; and

    (iii) that the collision occurred when the Claimant without warning ran from the northern pavement of the Strand into the road in front of the motorcycle.

    (b)   Save as aforesaid the paragraph is denied.

2. As to paragraph 2 of the Particulars of Claim, it is denied that the Defendant was negligent as alleged therein or at all, and the Defendant pleads to the Particulars of Negligence as follows:

   (a) *As to Particulars of Negligence (a)*

   There was no obligation to give way. The Claimant was not on the pedestrian crossing at the time of the collision, nor had he been on the pedestrian crossing immediately before the collision or at all to the knowledge of the Defendant.

   (b) *As to Particulars of Negligence (b) and (f)*

   It was impossible for the Defendant to stop or otherwise avoid the collision. The Defendant ran without warning into the path of the motorcycle.

   (c) *As to Particulars of Negligence (c)*

   Immediately before the collision, as soon as the Claimant ran into the road, the Defendant applied his brakes and this did slow the motorcycle, but not sufficiently to avoid the collision.

   (d) *As to Particulars of Negligence (d) and (e)*

   The Defendant was keeping a proper look out. He noticed the Claimant as soon as he ran into the road. The Claimant gave no warning whatever that he was about to do so.

   (e) *As to Particulars of Negligence (g)*

   The speed limit on the part of the road where the accident occurred, and on the approach to it, is 30 miles per hour. At no material time did the motorcycle go above 20 miles per hour, and at the time of the collision, because he braked immediately before the collision, the motorcycle was travelling at about 15 miles per hour.

3. The accident was caused or contributed to by the negligence of the Claimant.

PARTICULARS OF CLAIMANT'S NEGLIGENCE

(a)   Running into the road without giving any warning.

(b)   Failing to look right when entering the road, and so failing to see the motorcycle.

4. As to paragraph 3 of the Particulars of Claim:

(a)   The Defendant does not know about the alleged or any injuries, loss or damage, and therefore requires the Claimant to prove them.

(b)   Insofar as the allegation of causation is simply an assertion that the accident caused the injuries, this, for the reason set out in para 4(a) above, is not admitted.

(c)   Insofar as the allegation of causation is an assertion that the Defendant's pleaded negligence (rather than the accident itself) caused any injuries, this is denied.

5. No admissions are made as to the Claimant's entitlement to interest on any sum found due to him.

COUNTERCLAIM

6. Paragraphs 1 to 4 inclusive of the Defence are repeated.

7. By reason of the Claimant's said negligence the Defendant (who was born on 23 March 1954) was injured and the motorcycle was damaged, and by reason thereof the Defendant has suffered loss and damage.

PARTICULARS OF PERSONAL INJURIES

(a)   Left scaphoid fracture.

(b)   Bruising to the left shoulder.

(c)   The fracture healed uneventfully with conservative treatment within 9 months of the injury. The bruising caused pain for 2 weeks. No long term sequelae are expected.

(d)   Further details are set out in the report of Mr Smith, Consultant Orthopaedic Surgeon, dated 23 January 2001, a copy of which is annexed hereto.

PARTICULARS OF SPECIAL DAMAGES

Particulars are set out in a separate schedule annexed hereto.

8.   Further the Defendant is entitled to and counterclaims interest on the sum found due to him for such period and at such rate as the court may think fit, pursuant to s 69 of the County Courts Act 1984.

AND the Defendant counterclaims:

(a) damages;

(b) interest pursuant to statute as aforesaid.

O CROMWELL

STATEMENT OF TRUTH

I .... believe that the facts stated in this Defence and Counterclaim are true.

Signed ....

DATED this   Day of   2001

8.7 Reply and Defence to counterclaim

The response to the Defence and Counterclaim, above, 8.6.3.

IN THE CENTRAL LONDON COUNTY COURT **Claim No**

BETWEEN:

EDWARD CONFESSOR *Claimant*

and

WILLIAM CONQUEROR *Defendant*

REPLY AND DEFENCE TO COUNTERCLAIM

REPLY

1. The Particulars of Claim are repeated.

2. It is denied that the Claimant was negligent as alleged or at all, on the grounds that the accident occurred as pleaded in the Particulars of Claim.

DEFENCE TO COUNTERCLAIM

3. Paragraphs 1 and 2 of this Reply are repeated.

4. The Claimant has no knowledge of the pleaded or any personal injuries, loss or damage, and therefore requires the Defendant to prove:

    (a) all the pleaded personal injuries, loss and damage; and

    (b) that any personal injuries, loss or damage the Defendant may prove were caused by any negligence on the part of the Claimant that the Defendant may prove.

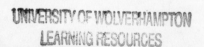

5. No admissions are made as to the Defendant's entitlement to interest on any sum found due to him.

STATEMENT OF TRUTH

I .... believe that the facts stated in this Reply and Defence to Counterclaim are true.

Signed ....

DATED this   Day of   2001

Bibliography and Further Reading

Adler, M
(1990)

Clarity for Lawyers: The Use of Plain English in Legal Writing
The Law Society

Burchfield, RW
(1998)

The New Fowler's Modern English Usage
3rd edn, Clarendon

Costanzo, M
(1994)

Legal Writing
Cavendish Publishing

Fowler, HW and Fowler, FG
(1996)

The King's English
3rd edn, OUP

Gerlis, SM and Loughlin, P
(2001)

Civil Procedure
Forthcoming, Cavendish Publishing

Gower, E (Sir)
(1987)

The Complete Plain Words
3rd edn, Penguin

James, JS *et al* (eds)
(1986)

Stroud's Judicial Dictionary
Sweet & Maxwell

Piesse, L and Smith, JG
(1965)

The Elements of Drafting
3rd edn, Stevens

Robinson, S
(1998)

Drafting
5th edn, Sweet & Maxwell

Rose, WM
(1999)

*Pleading Without Tears: A Guide
to Legal Drafting Under the
Civil Procedure Rules*
3rd edn, Blackstone

Rylance, P
(1994)

Legal Writing and Drafting
Blackstone

Thring, H (Baron)
(1902)

*Practical Legislation: The
Composition and Language of
Acts of Parliament and
Business Documents*
John Murray